300 Quotations for Preachers

300 QUOTATIONS FOR PREACHERS

Elliot Ritzema

Editor

300 Quotations for Preachers
Pastorum Series

Copyright 2013 Lexham Press.

Lexham Press, 1313 Commercial St., Bellingham, WA 98225
http://www.lexhampress.com

All Scripture quotations are from the Lexham English Bible (LEB). Copyright 2013 Lexham Press.

ISBN 978-1-57-799536-4

Publisher: John D. Barry
Associate Publishers: Michael R. Grigoni and Rebecca Kruyswijk
Assistant Editors: Rebecca Brant and Elizabeth Vince
Typesetting: projectluz.com
Cover Design: Jim LePage

Contents

Introduction

I love to share favorite quotations. They enable me to say what I want to say—better than I could say it myself. There's something about a well-turned phrase from a respected author that speaks deeply to people's hearts.

Many preachers have had the experience of trying to remember a quote that could make their message stick in the minds of their listeners. So they rack their brains, wondering where it was that Augustine talked about people's hearts being restless, or Charles Spurgeon made that comment about the gospel being like a lion, able to take care of itself if it is let out of its cage. Or was it the Bible being like a tiger? (See page 236 for the answer.)

This book aims to help preachers and other speakers by offering quotations from hundreds of years of church history from such leading writers and preachers as Richard Baxter, G. K. Chesterton, John Chrysostom, and Thomas à Kempis. Above each quotation are themes and Scripture references associated with that quotation; theme and Scripture indexes are in the back of the book. Quotations that use archaic language (like "thee" and "thou"), or words that have changed in meaning over time, have been updated. This makes them ready to use in a modern context.

It is my hope and prayer that this book will serve you well as you research a topic or Scripture, and as you share God's truth with others.

—Elliot Ritzema
Bellingham, Washington

Believing In Order to Understand

Hebrews 11:3

Theme: Faith, Wisdom

I do not seek to understand in order that I may believe, but I believe in order that I may understand; for of this I feel sure, that, if I did not believe, I would not understand.

—Anselm of Canterbury

Proslogium

Remind Yourself That You Are Going to Die

Psalm 39:4; 144:4; Ecclesiastes 6:12; 8:8

Theme: Death, Stress

Think day by day that you are going to die, and you will not fidget yourself about tomorrow.

—Anselm of Canterbury

Meditation 16

The Effect of God Illuminating the Mind

Ephesians 2:8; Hebrews 11:1

Theme: Faith

Faith is the effect of God illuminating the mind and sealing the heart, and it is his mere gift.

—James Arminius

Nine Questions, Q. vi

Be More Concerned with
What Happens After Death

2 Corinthians 5:1; Philippians 1:21

Theme: Death

That death is not to be judged an evil which is the end of a good life; for death becomes evil only by the retribution which follows it. They, then, who are destined to die, need not be careful to inquire what death they are to die, but into what place death will usher them.

—Augustine of Hippo
City of God, Chapter 11

Christ Made All Things New

Psalm 103:5; Revelation 21:5

Theme: Creation, Renewal of Creation, Birth of Jesus

He came when all things were growing old, and made them new. As a made, created, perishing thing, the world was now declining to its fall. It could not but be that it should abound in troubles; He came both to console you in the midst of present troubles, and to promise you everlasting rest. Do not choose then to cleave to this aged world, and to be unwilling to grow young in Christ.

—Augustine of Hippo
Sermon 31 on the New Testament

"Faith Ought to Go Before Understanding"

John 10:30; 17:21; Hebrews 11:3

Theme: Faith, Wisdom

You have heard what the Lord God, Jesus Christ, the Only Son of God, born of God the Father without any mother, and born of a Virgin mother without any human father, said, "I and My Father are One." Receive this, believe it in such a way that you may attain to understand it. For faith ought to go before understanding, that understanding may be the reward of faith.

—Augustine of Hippo

Sermon 89

No Mistakes in the Canonical Books of the Bible

2 Timothy 3:14–17; Hebrews 4:12

Theme: Scripture

For I acknowledge with high esteem for you, I have learned to ascribe such reverence and honor to those books of the Scriptures alone, which are now called canonical, that I believe most firmly that not one of their authors has made a mistake in writing them. And should I light upon anything in those writings, which may seem opposed to truth, I shall contend for nothing else, than either that the manuscript was full of errors, or that the translator had not comprehended what was said, or that I had not understood it in the least degree.

—Augustine of Hippo

Letter to Jerome

Not Too Much Service,
Not Too Much Contemplation

Deuteronomy 22:1; Matthew 22:39; Luke 3:11

Theme: Service, Discipline, Neighbors

No man has a right to lead such a life of contemplation as to forget in his own ease the service due to his neighbor; nor has any man a right to be so immersed in active life as to neglect the contemplation of God.

—Augustine of Hippo
City of God, Chapter 19

"Our Hearts Are Restless"

Matthew 11:29

Theme: Sabbath

You have formed us for yourself, and our hearts are restless till they find rest in you.

—Augustine of Hippo
Confessions, Book One

The Beginning of Good Works

Psalm 32:5; Proverbs 28:13; James 5:16; 1 John 1:9

Theme: Confession, Good Works, Evil, Repentance

The confession of evil works is the beginning of good works.

—Augustine of Hippo

Tractate 12 on the Gospel of John

The Depth of the Christian Scriptures

John 5:39

Theme: Scripture

Such is the depth of the Christian Scriptures, that even if I were attempting to study them and nothing else from early boyhood to decrepit old age, with the utmost leisure, the most unwearied zeal, and talents greater than I have, I would be still daily making progress in discovering their treasures.

—Augustine of Hippo

Letter to Volusianus

"Understanding Is the Reward of Faith"

Isaiah 7:9; 43:10; John 7:14–18

Theme: Faith, Wisdom

Understanding is the reward of faith.
Therefore do not seek to understand in
order to believe, but believe that you
may understand.

—Augustine of Hippo

Tractate 29 on the Gospel of John

You Hurt Yourself by Not Loving Enemies

Matthew 5:43–44; Luke 6:27–36

Theme: Love, Conflict

You have enemies. For who can live on this earth without them? Take heed to yourselves: love them. In no way can your enemy so hurt you by his violence, as you hurt yourself if you love him not.

—Augustine of Hippo

Sermon Six on the New Testament

A Little Philosophy Inclines
Man's Mind to Atheism

Psalm 14:1

Theme: Atheism, Philosophy

I had rather believe all the fables in the Legend, and the Talmud, and the Alcoran, than that this universal frame is without a mind. And therefore God never wrought a miracle to convince atheism, because his ordinary works convince it. It is true, that a little philosophy inclines man's mind to atheism; but depth in philosophy brings men's minds about to religion.

—Francis Bacon
Of Atheism

Virtue Is Like a Rich Stone

Proverbs 31:30

Theme: Beauty, Character

Virtue is like a rich stone, best plain set; and surely virtue is best in a body that is comely, though not of delicate features; and that has rather dignity of presence than beauty of aspect.

—Francis Bacon
Of Beauty

Bearing With Ministers' Vices
Damages the Church

Acts 20:28

Theme: Church Leadership

To bear with the vices of the ministers is to promote the ruin of the church. For what speedier way is there for the depraving and undoing of the people, than the depravity of their guides?

—Richard Baxter
The Reformed Pastor

Contend with Charity

Matthew 26:52; 1 Peter 3:9

Theme: Church Leadership, Love, Patience, Violence

If you believe that Christ was more worthy of imitation than Cæsar or Alexander; and that it is more glory to be a Christian than to be a conqueror, even to be a man than a beast, which often exceed us in strength; then contend with charity, and not with violence; and set meekness, and love, and patience against force; and not force against force.

—Richard Baxter
The Reformed Pastor

Disputing About the True Church

John 17:20–23; Romans 14:1–23

Theme: Nature of the Church, Church Fellowship and Unity, Conflict

---

For one sect to say, "Ours is the true church," and another to say, "No, but ours is the true church," is as mad as to dispute whether your hall, or kitchen, or parlor, or coal-house is your house; and for one to say, "This is the house," and another, "No, but it is that": when a child can tell them, that the best is but a part, and the house contains them all.

—Richard Baxter
Christian Directory

Dwelling On the Same Essentials of Christianity

Galatians 1:6–7

Theme: Gospel

I like to hear a man dwell much on the same essentials of Christianity. For we have but one God, and one Christ, and one faith to preach; and I will not preach another Gospel to please men with variety, as if our Savior and our Gospel were grown stale.

—Richard Baxter

Treatise of Conversion

How Can a Cold Heart Warm Others?

Acts 20:28

Theme: Church Leadership

A minister should take some special pains with his heart before he goes to the congregation: If it be then cold, how is it likely to warm the hearts of the hearers?

—Richard Baxter

The Reformed Pastor

Humility an Essential Part of the New Creature

Philippians 2:3

Theme: Humility

Humility is not a mere ornament of a Christian, but an essential part of the new creature. It is a contradiction to be a sanctified man, or a true Christian, and not humble.

—Richard Baxter
The Reformed Pastor

Make the Church's Wounds Your Own

2 Timothy 2:23

Theme: Conflict, Church Fellowship and Unity

How rare is it to meet with a man that smarts or bleeds with the Church's wounds, or sensibly takes them to heart as his own; or that ever had eager thoughts of a cure! No, but almost every party thinks that the happiness of the rest consists only in turning to them; and because they are not of their mind, they cry, "Down with them," and are glad to hear of their fall, thinking that is the way to the Church's rising— that is, their own. How few are there that understand the true state of controversies between the several parties; or that ever well discerned how many of them are but verbal, and how many are real!

—Richard Baxter
The Reformed Pastor

Many Doctrinal Differences Must Be Tolerated

Mark 3:25; Romans 16:17; Hebrews 12:14

Theme: Peace, Conflict, Church Fellowship and Unity

He that is not a son of peace, is not a son of God. All other sins destroy the church consequentially, but division and separation demolish it directly. Building the church is but an orderly joining of the materials; and what then is disjoining, but pulling down? Many doctrinal differences must be tolerated in a church. And why, but for unity and peace? Therefore, disunion and separation is utterly intolerable.

—Richard Baxter

The Saints' Everlasting Rest

Most Mischiefs Caused By Families

1 Timothy 3:4; 5:4–8

Theme: Family

It is an evident truth, that most of the mischiefs that now infest or seize upon mankind throughout the earth, consist in, or are caused by, the disorders and ill-governedness of families.

—Richard Baxter
A Christian Directory

No Service Without Self-Denial

1 Corinthians 9:24–27

Theme: Church Leadership, Discipline

Self-denial is of absolute necessity in every Christian, but of a double necessity in a minister, as he has a double sanctification or dedication to God. Without self-denial he cannot do God an hour's faithful service. Hard studies, much knowledge, and excellent preaching are but more glorious and hypocritical sinning, if the end be not right.

—Richard Baxter
The Reformed Pastor

Prayer as Well as Preaching

Philippians 1:4; Colossians 1:3; 2 Thessalonians 1:11

Theme: Church Leadership, Prayer

Prayer must carry on our work as well as preaching; he does not preach heartily to his people who will not pray for them. If we do not prevail with God to give them faith and repentance, we are unlikely to prevail with them to believe and repent.

—Richard Baxter

The Reformed Pastor

Study of Scripture Needed

Acts 8:27–35

Theme: Scripture, Holy Spirit

It is not the work of the Spirit to tell you the meaning of Scripture, and give you the knowledge of divinity, without your own study and labor, but to bless that study, and give you knowledge thereby.

—Richard Baxter
The Unreasonableness of Infidelity

Take Heed Lest Your Example
Contradict Your Doctrine

Leviticus 19:14; Acts 20:28

Theme: Church Leadership, Character

Take heed to yourselves, lest your example contradict your doctrine, and lest you lay such stumbling blocks before the blind as may be the occasion of their ruin; lest you may unsay that with your lives which you say with your tongues; and be the greatest hinderers of the success of your own labors.

—Richard Baxter

The Reformed Pastor

The Good of Contempt for the World

2 Timothy 4:10

Theme: Church Leadership, Hypocrisy

O what abundance of good might ministers do if they would but live in a contempt of the world, and the riches and glory of it, and expend all they have for their Master's use. This would unlock more hearts to the reception of their doctrine than all their oratory will do; and without this, singularity in religion will seem but hypocrisy, and it is likely that it is so.

—Richard Baxter

The Reformed Pastor

The Necessity of Speaking Truth Plainly

Ecclesiastes 12:10; John 3:21

Theme: Truth, Speech

Truth overcomes prejudice by mere light of evidence, and there is no better way to make a good cause prevail than to make it as plain, and commonly, and thoroughly known as we can; and it is this light that will dispose an unprepared mind. At best it is a sign that he has not well digested the matter himself, who is not able to deliver it plainly to another.

—Richard Baxter

The Reformed Pastor

The Unexpected Pains of Becoming More Holy

Malachi 3:1–3

Theme: Holiness

Reformation is to many of us, as the Messiah was to the Jews. Before he came they looked and longed for him, and boasted of him, and rejoiced in hope of him; but when he came, they hated him, and would not believe that he was indeed the Person, and therefore persecuted and put him to death, to the curse and confusion of the main body of their nation. …

So it is with too many about reformation. They hoped for a reformation that should bring them more wealth and honor with the people, and power to force men to do what they would have them; and now they see a reformation that must put them to more condescension and pains than ever they were at before; this will not go down with them.

—Richard Baxter

The Reformed Pastor

Unite In Necessary Truths

Acts 15:6–29

Theme: Church Fellowship and Unity, Peace

I would recommend to all my brethren, as the most necessary thing to the Church's peace, that you unite in necessary truths, and tolerate tolerable failings; and bear with one another in things that may be borne with; and do not make a larger creed and more necessaries than God has done.

—Richard Baxter
The Reformed Pastor

Your Congregations Are the Purchase of Christ's Blood

Acts 20:28

Theme: Church Leadership

Every time we look upon our congregations, let us believingly remember that they are the purchase of Christ's blood, and therefore should be regarded accordingly by us.

—Richard Baxter
The Reformed Pastor

"Christic Is the Morning Star"

Revelation 2:28; 22:16

Theme: Jesus, Eternity

Christ is the morning star, who promises and reveals to the saints the eternal light of life, when the night of the world is past.

—Venerable Bede

Exposition of the Apocalypse

God Loved You Before and Loves You More

John 3:16; Romans 5:8; Ephesians 2:4–5; 1 John 4:10

Theme: Love of God

He loves you more than you love Him,
and He loved you before you loved Him.

—Bernard of Clairvaux

Fragment on the Song of Songs

"A World in a Grain of Sand"

Psalm 8:3–9

Theme: Creation

To see a world in a grain of sand,
And a heaven in a wild flower,
Hold infinity in the palm of your hand,
And eternity in an hour.

—William Blake
Auguries of Innocence

Jesus More Than a Man

John 13:34–35; 15:12, 17

Theme: Divinity of Jesus, Love of God, Scripture

I know men, and I tell you Jesus Christ was not a man. Superficial minds see a resemblance between Christ and the founders of empires and the gods of other religions. That resemblance does not exist. There is between Christianity and other religions the distance of infinity. Alexander, Cæsar, Charlemagne and myself founded empires. But on what did we rest the creations of our genius? Upon sheer force. Jesus Christ alone founded His empire upon love; and at this hour millions of men will die for Him.

—Napoleon Bonaparte
Discussion with Count de Motholon

'Twas I That Did It

Matthew 27:11–44; Mark 15:1–32; Luke 23:1–43; John 19:1–24

Theme: Death of Jesus

I see the crowd in Pilate's hall,
I mark their wrathful mien;
Their shouts of "crucify" appall,
With blasphemy between.
And of that shouting multitude
I feel that I am one;
And in that din of voices rude,
I recognise my own. …
'Twas I that shed the sacred blood,
I nailed him to the tree,
I crucified the Christ of God,
I joined the mockery.
Yet not the less that blood avails,
To cleanse away my sin,
And not the less that cross prevails
To give me peace within.

—Horatius Bonar
'Twas I That Did It

Prayer in the Morning

Mark 1:35

Theme: Prayer

The men who have done the most for God in this world have been early on their knees. He who fritters away the early morning, its opportunity and freshness, in other pursuits than seeking God will make poor headway seeking him the rest of the day. If God is not first in our thoughts and efforts in the morning, he will be in the last place the remainder of the day.

—E. M. Bounds
Power Through Prayer

What the Church Needs Is Prayer

Luke 18:1; Ephesians 6:18; 1 Thessalonians 5:17

Theme: Prayer, Church

What the Church needs today is not more machinery or better, not new organizations or more and novel methods, but men whom the Holy Ghost can use—men of prayer, men mighty in prayer. The Holy Ghost does not flow through methods, but through men. He does not come on machinery, but on men. He does not anoint plans, but men—men of prayer.

—E. M. Bounds

Power Through Prayer

Not Hasty Reading, but Meditating

Psalm 19:14; 119:148

Theme: Scripture

Remember, it is not hasty reading, but serious meditating upon holy and heavenly truths, that makes them prove sweet and profitable to the soul. It is not the bee's touching of the flower that gathers honey, but her abiding for a time upon the flower that draws out the sweet. It is not he that reads most, but he that meditates most, that will prove the choicest, sweetest, wisest, and strongest Christian.

—Thomas Brooks

Precious Remedies

One Lamb Worrying Another

2 Corinthians 12:20; Galatians 5:19–21

Theme: Conflict, Church Fellowship and Unity

Discord and division become no Christian. For wolves to worry the lambs, is no wonder; but for one lamb to worry another, this is unnatural and monstrous.

—Thomas Brooks

Precious Remedies

The Importance of Action for Being a Christian

1 Samuel 15:22

Theme: Obedience

When Demosthenes was asked what was the first part of an orator, what the second, what the third, he answered: *Action*. The same may I say, if any should ask me what is the first, the second, the third part of a Christian, I must answer: *Action*.

—Thomas Brooks

The Unsearchable Riches of Christ

The Soul Lives By Believing

2 Corinthians 5:7

Theme: Faith

It will never be well with you so long as you are swayed by carnal reason, and rely more upon your five senses than the four evangelists. … As the body lives by breathing, so the soul lives by believing.

—Thomas Brooks

The Unsearchable Riches of Christ

"A Saint Abroad and a Devil at Home"

Ephesians 5:25–33; 6:4; Colossians 3:19, 21

Theme: Fathers, Husbands, Hypocrisy, Family

I have been in his family, and have observed him both at home and abroad; and I know what I say of him is the truth. His house is as empty of religion, as the white of an egg is of savour. … Thus say the common people that know him, "A saint abroad, and a devil at home."

—John Bunyan
The Pilgrim's Progress

Go Forward into Death

Psalm 23:4; Revelation 2:10

Theme: Death, Fear, Courage

To go back is nothing but death; to go forward is fear of death, and life everlasting beyond it. I will yet go forward.

—John Bunyan

The Pilgrim's Progress

"He That Is Down Needs Fear No Fall"

Philippians 4:12–13; Hebrews 13:5

Theme: Contentment, Humility

He that is down needs fear no fall;
He that is low, no pride;
He that is humble, ever shall
Have God to be his guide.
I am content with what I have,
Little be it, or much;
And, Lord, contentment still I crave,
Because Thou savest such.
Fullness to such a burden is,
That go on pilgrimage;
Here little, and hereafter bliss,
Is best from age to age.

—John Bunyan
The Pilgrim's Progress

The Beginning of John Bunyan's Conversion

Numbers 23:9; Matthew 18:3

Theme: Conversion

I came where there were three or four poor women sitting at a door in the sun, and talking about the things of God. … Their talk was about a new birth, the work of God on their hearts, also how they were convinced of their miserable state by nature; they talked how God had visited their souls with his love in the Lord Jesus, and with what words and promises they had been refreshed, comforted, and supported against the temptations of the devil.

And I thought they spoke … with such pleasantness of Scripture language, and with such appearance of grace in all they said, that they were to me, as if they had found a new world.

—John Bunyan
Grace Abounding to the Chief of Sinners

"Grief Should Be the Instructor of the Wise"

Ecclesiastes 1:18

Theme: Grief, Wisdom

Grief should be the instructor of the wise;
Sorrow is knowledge: they who know the most
Must mourn the deepest o'er the fatal truth,
The Tree of Knowledge is not that of Life.

—Lord Byron
Manfred

Jesus Christ Both God and Man

John 1:14

Theme: Divinity of Jesus, Humanity of Jesus

If ever man was God, or God man, Jesus Christ was both.

—Lord Byron

A Dog Barks When He Sees His Master Attacked

2 Timothy 1:7; 4:1–8

Theme: Obedience, Courage

A dog will bark if he sees his master attacked, and I should be a cowardly wretch if I could see God's truth assailed and stood by silent.

—John Calvin

Letter to Margaret of Navarre

A Pilot Steers Our Ship

Genesis 15:1; Joshua 1:9; Psalm 56:4; Matthew 10:28;
Luke 12:4; 1 Peter 3:14

Theme: Suffering, Fear, Stress

Although we may be severely buffeted hither and thither by many tempests, yet, seeing that a pilot steers the ship in which we sail, who will never allow us to perish even in the midst of shipwrecks, there is no reason why our minds should be overwhelmed with fear and overcome with weariness.

—John Calvin

Letter to Farel

Calvin on the Death of His Wife

Matthew 5:4; John 11:31, 33

Theme: Grief

Although the death of my wife has been exceedingly painful to me, yet I subdue my grief as well as I can. Friends, also, are earnest in their duty to me. It might be wished, indeed, that they could profit me and themselves more; yet one can scarcely say how much I am supported by their attentions. But you know well enough how tender, or rather soft, my mind is. Had not a powerful self-control, therefore, been vouchsafed to me, I could not have borne up so long.

—John Calvin

Letter to Viret

Faith Alone Justifies, but Is Not Alone

Romans 3:22; Galatians 5:6

Theme: Faith, Justification

It is ... faith alone which justifies, and yet the faith which justifies is not alone.

—John Calvin

Antidote to the Canons of the Council of Trent, Canon XI

Marks of the Church

Matthew 18:20

Theme: Church, Nature of the Church, Presence of God

Wherever we find the word of God purely preached and heard, and the sacraments administered according to the institution of Christ; there, it is not to be doubted, is a Church of God: for his promise can never deceive: "Where two or three are gathered together in my name, there am I in the midst of them."

—John Calvin
Institutes, Book Four

Not Sure About Guardian Angels

Daniel 12:1; Acts 12:15

Theme: Angels

Whether or not each believer has a single angel assigned to him for his defense, I dare not positively affirm.

—John Calvin

Institutes, Book One

Prepare for a Hard Life

Hebrews 12:6

Theme: Suffering

Those whom the Lord has chosen and honored with his fellowship must prepare for a hard, laborious, troubled life, a life full of many and various kinds of evils; it being the will of our heavenly Father to exercise his people in this way while putting them to the proof. Having begun this course with Christ the first-born, he continues it towards all his children.

—John Calvin
Institutes, Book Three

Refraining from Speculation About Angels

Colossians 2:18

Theme: Angels

If we would be duly wise, we must renounce those vain babblings of idle men, concerning the nature, ranks, and number of angels, without any authority from the Word of God. I know that many fasten on these topics more eagerly, and take greater pleasure in them than in those relating to daily practice. But if we decline not to be the disciples of Christ, let us not decline to follow the method which he has prescribed. In this way, being contented with him for our master, we will not only refrain from, but even feel averse to, superfluous speculations which he discourages.

—John Calvin

Institutes, Book One

The Accommodation of God

Hebrews 1:1–4

Theme: Revelation

God cannot be comprehended by us, unless as far as he accommodates himself to our standard.

—John Calvin
Lecture 23 on Ezekiel

The Necessity of Depending on God

Genesis 17:1; Psalm 62:7; Isaiah 50:10; Hosea 12:6

Theme: Faith

There is no other method of living
piously and justly, than that of depending
upon God.

—John Calvin
Commentary on Genesis

True Meaning of Scripture Is the Natural Meaning

Acts 8:26–31; Galatians 4:21–25

Theme: Scripture

Let us know, then, that the true meaning of Scripture is the natural and obvious meaning; and let us embrace and abide by it resolutely. Let us not only neglect as doubtful, but boldly set aside as deadly corruptions, those pretended expositions, which lead us away from the natural meaning.

—John Calvin
Commentary on Galatians

We Are Not Our Own; We Are God's

1 Corinthians 6:19–20; 7:23

Theme: Commitment

We are not our own; therefore, neither our reason nor our will should predominate in our deliberations and actions. We are not our own; therefore let us not propose it as our end, to seek what may be expedient for us according to the flesh. We are not our own; therefore let us, as far as possible, forget ourselves and all things that are ours. On the contrary, we are God's; to him therefore let us live and die. We are God's; therefore let his wisdom and will preside in all our actions. We are God's; towards him therefore, as our only legitimate end, let every part of our lives be directed.

—John Calvin

Institutes, Book Three

"Jesus Is Our Divinest Symbol"

Colossians 1:15–17

Theme: Jesus

Jesus is our divinest symbol. Higher has the human thought not yet reached. A symbol of quite perennial, infinite character: whose significance will ever demand to be anew inquired into and anew made manifest.

—Thomas Carlyle

Sartor Resartus

Theologically Knowing and Spiritually Ignorant

1 Corinthians 8:1; 13:2

Theme: Wisdom, Education

A man may be theologically knowing and spiritually ignorant.

—Stephen Charnock
A Discourse on the Knowledge of God

America Founded on a Creed

2 Peter 2:13–17

Theme: Government, Justice

America is the only nation in the world that is founded on a creed. That creed is set forth with dogmatic and even theological lucidity in the Declaration of Independence; perhaps the only piece of practical politics that is also theoretical politics and also great literature. It enunciates that all men are equal in their claim to justice, that governments exist to give them that justice, and that their authority is for that reason just. It certainly does condemn anarchism, and it does also by inference condemn atheism, since it clearly names the Creator as the ultimate authority from whom these equal rights are derived.

—G. K. Chesterton
What I Saw in America

Believing in Christianity Upon the Evidence

John 6:29–30; Hebrews 11:1–3

Theme: Faith, Doubt

If I am asked, as a purely intellectual question, why I believe in Christianity, I can only answer, "For the same reason that an intelligent agnostic disbelieves in Christianity." I believe in it quite rationally upon the evidence. But the evidence in my case, as in that of the intelligent agnostic, is not really in this or that alleged demonstration; it is in an enormous accumulation of small but unanimous facts.

—G. K. Chesterton

Orthodoxy

Conviction Not Responsible for Bigotry

Matthew 5:46–47; Luke 18:11

Theme: Prejudice

A common hesitation in our day touching the use of extreme convictions is a sort of notion that extreme convictions, especially upon cosmic matters, have been responsible in the past for the thing which is called bigotry. But a very small amount of direct experience will dissipate this view. In real life the people who are most bigoted are the people who have no convictions at all.

—G.K. Chesterton

Heretics

Doubtful About Truth, Undoubting About Self

Matthew 14:31; 28:17; Luke 24:38; John 20:27

Theme: Doubt, Truth

A man was meant to be doubtful about himself, but undoubting about the truth; this has been exactly reversed.

—G. K. Chesterton

Orthodoxy

Faith Is Unfashionable

1 Corinthians 13:13; Hebrews 11:1

Theme: Faith

Faith is unfashionable, and it is customary on every side to cast against it the fact that it is a paradox. Everybody mockingly repeats the famous childish definition that faith is "the power of believing that which we know to be untrue." Yet it is not one atom more paradoxical than hope or charity. Charity is the power of defending that which we know to be indefensible. Hope is the power of being cheerful in circumstances which we know to be desperate.

—G. K. Chesterton

Heretics

"I Am Not Myself"

Genesis 3:6; 1 Corinthians 15:22; 2 Corinthians 11:3

Theme: Sin

To the question, "What are you?" I could only answer, "God knows." To the question, "What is meant by the Fall?" I could answer with complete sincerity, "That whatever I am, I am not myself."

—G. K. Chesterton

Orthodoxy

Most Modern Freedom Is Fear

John 8:31–36

Theme: Freedom, Responsibility

Most modern freedom is at root fear. It is not so much that we are too bold to endure rules; it is rather that we are too timid to endure responsibilities.

—G. K. Chesterton
What's Wrong With the World

"The Christian Ideal Has Not Been Tried"

Matthew 16:24; Mark 8:34; Luke 9:23; 14:27

Theme: Discipleship

The Christian ideal has not been tried and found wanting. It has been found difficult; and left untried.

—G. K. Chesterton

What's Wrong With the World

The Need to Face Actions Fully

Matthew 12:36–37

Theme: Responsibility

Both men and women ought to face more fully the things they do or cause to be done; face them or leave off doing them.

—G. K. Chesterton
What's Wrong With the World

Don't Let Tares Force You to Withdraw from the Church

Matthew 3:12; 13:24–30; 2 Timothy 2:20

Theme: Church Fellowship and Unity

Although there seem to be tares in the Church, yet neither our faith nor our charity ought to be hindered, so that because we see that there are tares in the Church we ourselves should withdraw from the Church. We ought only to labor that we may be wheat, that when the wheat shall begin to be gathered into the Lord's barns, we may receive fruit for our labor and work. Let us strive, dearest brethren, and labor as much as we possibly can, that we may be vessels of gold or silver. But to the Lord alone it is granted to break the vessels of earth, to whom also is given the rod of iron.

—Cyprian of Carthage

Letter to the Roman Confessors

God as Father and Church as Mother

Matthew 16:18

Theme: Church

He can no longer have God for his Father, who has not the Church for his mother.

—Cyprian of Carthage
On the Unity of the Church

No Statements About the Faith
Without the Scriptures

Acts 17:10–11

Theme: Scripture

Concerning the divine and holy mysteries of the Faith, not even a casual statement must be delivered without the Holy Scriptures; nor must we be drawn aside by mere plausibility and artifices of speech. Even to me, who tells you these things, give not absolute credence, unless you receive the proof of the things which I announce from the Divine Scriptures.

—Cyril of Jerusalem

Catechetical Lecture on the Ten Points of Doctrine

Good to Be a Child at Christmas

Luke 2:7

Theme: Birth of Jesus, Children

It is good to be children sometimes, and never better than at Christmas, when its mighty Founder was a child himself.

—Charles Dickens

A Christmas Carol

Death Be Not Proud

1 Corinthians 15:26
Theme: Death

Death, be not proud, though some have callèd thee
Mighty and dreadful, for thou art not so:
For those whom thou think'st thou dost overthrow
Die not, poor Death; nor yet canst thou kill me. …
One short sleep past, we wake eternally,
And Death shall be no more: Death, thou shalt die!

—John Donne
Death Be Not Proud

Death Comes to Us All

Ecclesiastes 3:19; 7:2; 1 Corinthians 15:26

Theme: Death

Death comes equally to us all and makes us all equal when it comes.

—John Donne

Lenten Sermon on First Corinthians

Afraid to Take a New Step

Luke 12:5

Theme: Fear

It would be interesting to know what it is men are most afraid of. Taking a new step, uttering a new word is what they fear most.

—Fyodor Dostoyevsky

Crime and Punishment

Christ Like a River

Isaiah 32:2; John 4:10–14; 7:38; Ephesians 4:15–16

Theme: Jesus

Christ is like a river. … A river is continually flowing, there are fresh supplies of water coming from the fountain-head continually, so that a man may live by it, and be supplied with water all his life. So Christ is an ever-flowing fountain; he is continually supplying his people, and the fountain is not spent. They who live upon Christ, may have fresh supplies from him to all eternity; they may have an increase of blessedness that is new, and new still, and which never will come to an end.

—Jonathan Edwards

Sermon on Isaiah

Counterfeits Are No Argument Against Truth

Matthew 7:15–20; 2 Timothy 3:8; 2 Peter 2:1; 1 John 4:1–3

Theme: Revival, False Teaching

That there are some counterfeits, is no argument that nothing is true: such things are always expected in a time of reformation. If we look into church history, we shall find no instance of any great revival of religion, but what has been attended with many such things.

—Jonathan Edwards

Marks of a Work of the True Spirit

False Prophets Incorrigible in Their Misconduct

Jeremiah 23:13–29; 2 Peter 2:1

Theme: Revelation, Pride, Guidance, False Teaching

As long as a person has a notion that he is guided by immediate direction from heaven, it makes him incorrigible and impregnable in all his misconduct.

—Jonathan Edwards

Thoughts on the Revival of Religion in New England

"If It Were the Last Hour of My Life"

Ephesians 5:16; Colossians 4:5

Theme: Wisdom, Responsibility, Commitment

---

*R*esolved, Never to do anything which I should be afraid to do if it were the last hour of my life.

—Jonathan Edwards

Resolutions

Jonathan Edwards' Conversion

John 3:3–6; Ephesians 4:22–24

Theme: Conversion

On January 12, 1723, I made a solemn dedication of myself to God, and wrote it down; giving up myself, and all that I had, to God; to be for the future in no respect my own; to act as one that had no right to himself, in any respect. And solemnly vowed to take God for my whole portion and felicity, looking on nothing else as any part of my happiness, nor acting as it were; and his law for the constant rule of my obedience; engaging to fight with all my might against the world, the flesh, and the devil, to the end of my life.

—Jonathan Edwards

Memoirs

No Manifestation of God Without Difficulties

Isaiah 8:14; Romans 9:32–33; 1 Peter 2:8

Theme: Revelation, Scripture

There never yet was any great manifestation that God made of himself to the world, without many difficulties attending it. It is with the works of God, as with his word: they seem at first full of things that are strange, inconsistent, and difficult to the carnal unbelieving hearts of men.

—Jonathan Edwards
Marks of a Work of the True Spirit

The Devil Can Counterfeit the Spirit

1 Peter 5:8; 1 John 4:1–3

Theme: Devil, False Teaching

The devil can counterfeit all the saving operations and graces of the Spirit of God.

—Jonathan Edwards

A Treatise Concerning Religious Affections

Circumstances Can't Repair Character

Mark 7:21–23

Theme: Character

No change of circumstances can repair a defect of character.

—Ralph Waldo Emerson

Character

"Always Do What You Are Afraid to Do"

Joshua 1:6–9; Psalm 27:1–3

Theme: Courage

It was a high counsel that I once heard given to a young person, "Always do what you are afraid to do."

—Ralph Waldo Emerson

Heroism

Faith Comes in Moments

Romans 10:17

Theme: Faith

There is a difference between one and another hour of life in their authority and subsequent effect. Our faith comes in moments; our vice is habitual. Yet there is a depth in those brief moments which constrains us to ascribe more reality to them than to all other experiences.

—Ralph Waldo Emerson

The Over-Soul

What Distinguishes Christians from Other People

Matthew 5:11; John 15:20; 16:33; 2 Corinthians 4:12; 6:9–10; 10:3;
Philippians 3:20; 1 Peter 2:11

Theme: Discipleship, Sanctity of Life, Persecution

The Christians are distinguished from other men neither by country, nor language, nor the customs which they observe. For they neither inhabit cities of their own, nor employ a peculiar form of speech. … They dwell in their own countries, but simply as sojourners. As citizens, they share in all things with others, and yet endure all things as if foreigners. Every foreign land is to them as their native country, and every land of their birth as a land of strangers. They marry, as do all [others]; they beget children, but they do not destroy their offspring. They have a common table, but not a common bed.

—*Epistle to Diognetus*

Revivals Are New Beginnings of Obedience

Psalm 85:6; Hosea 6:2

Theme: Revival, Obedience

A revival is nothing else than a new beginning of obedience to God.

—Charles Finney

Lecture One on Revivals of Religion

Christians Are Gold in the Ore

1 John 3:2

Theme: Death

A Christian in this world is but gold in the ore; at death, the pure gold is melted out and separated, and the dross cast away and consumed.

—John Flavel

A Treatise on the Soul of Man

Controversies and Sap Suckers

1 Timothy 1:4; Titus 3:9; Hebrews 13:9

Theme: Conflict

Many controversies of these times grow up about religion, as suckers from the root and limbs of a fruit-tree, which spend the vital sap that should make it fruitful.

—John Flavel

The Causes and Cures of Mental Errors

Do Not Be Divided Unnecessarily

Matthew 5:24; Romans 16:17; 1 Corinthians 1:10; 11:18; 12:25;

Titus 3:10; Jude 19

Theme: Conflict, Church Fellowship and Unity

Be deeply affected with the mischievous effects and consequences of schisms and divisions in the societies of the saints, and let nothing beneath a plain necessity divide you from communion one with another; hold it fast till you can hold it no longer without sin. At the fire of your contentions your enemies warm their hands, and say, "Aha, so would we have it."

—John Flavel
A Sermon on Gospel Unity

Entertaining Devils Unawares

Colossians 2:8; 1 Timothy 4:2–3; 2 Timothy 2:16–18; 4:3;
Hebrews 13:2, 9; 2 Peter 2:1–2

Theme: False Teaching

By entertaining of strange persons, men sometimes entertain angels unawares; but by entertaining of strange doctrines, many have entertained devils unawares.

—John Flavel
The Causes and Cures of Mental Errors

We Never Think Our Anger Is Unjust

Ephesians 4:26

Theme: Anger

There was never an angry man that thought his anger unjust.

—Francis de Sales

Introduction to the Devout Life

Belief in the Bible Has Guided Me

Psalm 119:105; Hebrews 4:12

Theme: Scripture, Guidance

It is a belief in the Bible which has served me as the guide of my moral and literary life. No criticism will be able to perplex the confidence which we have entertained of a writing whose contents have stirred up and given life to our vital energy by its own. The farther the ages advance in civilization the more will the Bible be used.

—Johann Wolfgang von Goethe
Personal Conversation

"Love Governed God"

Ephesians 2:4–6

Theme: Love of God, Death of Jesus

The poets themselves said that *amor Deum gubernat*, that love governed God. And, as Nazianzen well speaks, this love of God, this *dulcis tyrannus*—this sweet tyrant—did overcome him when he was upon the cross. There were no cords could have held him to the whipping-post but those of love; no nails have fastened him to the cross but those of love.

—Thomas Goodwin

Sermon 11 on the Second Chapter of Ephesians

Do Not Worry About the Time of Your Conversion

John 3:3–6; 2 Corinthians 5:17; Ephesians 4:22–24

Theme: Conversion, Temptation

Satan will ask the Christian what was the time of his conversion; "Are you a Christian," will he say, "and do you not know when you commenced?" Now keep the plains, and content yourself with this, that you see the streams of grace, though the time of your conversion be like the head of Nilus, not to be found. God often comes early, before gross sins have deflowered the soul, and steals into the creature's bosom without much noise. In such a case Satan does but abuse you, when he sends you on his errand. You may know the sun is up, though you did not observe when it rose.

—William Gurnall
The Christian in Complete Armour

False Doctrines Don't Agree

1 Thessalonians 5:21; 1 John 4:1

Theme: Scripture, False Teaching

Compare scripture with scripture. False doctrines, like false witnesses, agree not among themselves.

—William Gurnall

The Christian in Complete Armour

Peace of Conscience and Pardoning Mercy

Micah 7:18

Theme: Peace, Forgiveness, Mercy

Peace of conscience is nothing but the echo of pardoning mercy.

—William Gurnall

The Christian in Complete Armour

Praying for Truth Better Than Contending About It

John 18:37–38; Romans 15:30

Theme: Truth, Conflict, Prayer

We stand at better advantage to find truth, and keep it also, when devoutly praying for it, than fiercely wrangling and contending about it: disputes toil the soul, and raise the dust of passion; prayer sweetly composes the mind, and lays the passions which disputes draw forth; and I am sure a man may see further in a still, clear day, than in a windy and cloudy.

—William Gurnall

The Christian in Complete Armour

The Gospel Does Not Allow Fire Spitting

Matthew 5:43–44; 18:15–20; Luke 6:27, 35; James 4:1–2

Theme: Church Fellowship and Unity, Conflict, Peace

If the gospel will not allow us to pay our enemies in their own coin, and give them wrath for wrath, then much less will it suffer brethren to spit fire at one another's face.

—William Gurnall
The Christian in Complete Armour

Your Only Comfort in Life and Death

Matthew 10:29–31; Luke 21:18; John 6:39; 8:34–36; 10:28; Romans 8:28;
14:7–8; 1 Corinthians 3:23; 6:19; 2 Thessalonians 3:3; Titus 2:14;
Hebrews 2:14; 1 Peter 1:5, 18–19; 1 John 1:7; 2:2; 3:8

Theme: Comfort, Atonement

Q: What is your only comfort in life and death?

A: That I with body and soul, both in life and death, am not my own, but belong unto my faithful Savior Jesus Christ; who, with his precious blood, has fully satisfied for all my sins, and delivered me from all the power of the devil; and so preserves me that without the will of my heavenly Father, not a hair can fall from my head.

—The Heidelberg Catechism

"Sanctified Afflictions Are Spiritual Promotions"

Genesis 7:17–18

Theme: Suffering

Observe, 1. The waters which broke down everything else bore up the ark. That which to unbelievers is a savour of death unto death is to the faithful a savour of life unto life. 2. The more the waters increased, the higher the ark was lifted up towards heaven. Thus sanctified afflictions are spiritual promotions; and as troubles abound consolations much more abound.

—Matthew Henry

Matthew Henry's Commentary on the Whole Bible

Conditions of Membership and Salvation

Romans 15:7

Theme: Church Fellowship and Unity, Salvation

A Church has no right to make anything a condition of membership which Christ has not made a condition of salvation.

—A. A. Hodge

A Commentary on the Confession of Faith

Scripture Writers Ignorant of the Timing of the Second Coming

Matthew 24:36; Mark 13:32; 1 Corinthians 15:51

Theme: Scripture, Second Coming

The plenary inspiration of the sacred writers rendered them infallible in all they taught; but it did not render them omniscient. They could not err in what they communicated, but they might err, and doubtless did err, as to things not included in the communications of the Spirit. The time of the second advent was not revealed to them. They profess their ignorance on that point. They were, therefore, as to that matter, on a level with other men, and may have differed in regard to their private conjectures on the subject just as others differ.

—Charles Hodge

An Exposition of the First Epistle to the Corinthians

Source of Life, Sum of Excellence, Fullness of Joy

Romans 6:2–11

Theme: Union with Christ, Discipleship, Holiness

To be in Christ is the source of the Christian's life; to be like Christ is the sum of his excellence; to be with Christ is the fullness of his joy.

—Charles Hodge

A Commentary on the Epistle to the Romans

"Superstition Is Belief Without Evidence"

1 Kings 20:23; Isaiah 2:6

Theme: Superstition

Superstition is belief without evidence.

—Charles Hodge
Systematic Theology

Richard Hooker's Last Words

Psalm 102:11; 144:4

Theme: Death

God has heard my daily petitions, for I am at peace with all men, and He is at peace with me; and from that blessed assurance I feel that inward joy, which this world can neither give nor take from me: my conscience bears me this witness, and this witness makes the thoughts of death joyful. I could wish to live to do the Church more service, but cannot hope it, for my days are past as a shadow that returns not.

—Richard Hooker

Belief Requires a Miracle

Luke 16:31; Acts 8:13

Theme: Miracles

The Christian religion not only was at first attended with miracles, but even at this day cannot be believed by any reasonable person without one.

—David Hume

An Enquiry Concerning Human Understanding

"Let Me Attain to Jesus Christ"

Philippians 3:7–11

Theme: Persecution, Commitment, Death, Suffering

Let fire and the cross; let the crowds of wild beasts; let tearings, breakings, and dislocations of bones; let cutting off of members; let shatterings of the whole body; and let all the dreadful torments of the devil come upon me: only let me attain to Jesus Christ.

—Ignatius of Antioch
Letter to the Romans

"The Glory of God Is a Living Man"

Genesis 32:30; 2 Corinthians 3:18

Theme: Glory of God, Revelation

The glory of God is a living man; and the life of man consists in beholding God. For if the manifestation of God which is made by means of the creation affords life to all living in the earth, how much more does that revelation of the Father which comes through the Word give life to those who see God.

—Irenaeus of Lyons

Against Heresies

Examine Yourself Before Taking on Leadership

Luke 14:28; James 3:1

Theme: Church Leadership, Leadership

No one would venture to undertake the building of a house were he not an architect, nor will any one attempt the cure of sick bodies who is not a skilled physician; but even though many urge him, will beg off, and will not be ashamed to own his ignorance; and shall he who is going to have the care of so many souls entrusted to him, not examine himself beforehand?

—John Chrysostom

Treatise Concerning the Christian Priesthood

Novices, Not the Young,
Excluded from the Ministry

1 Timothy 4:12

Theme: Church Leadership

The young man ought not to be absolutely excluded from the ministry, but only the novice: and the difference between the two is great.

—John Chrysostom

Treatise Concerning the Christian Priesthood

Two Dangers of Preaching

Colossians 4:6

Theme: Church Leadership, Pride

If a preacher be indifferent to praise, and yet cannot produce the doctrine "which is with grace seasoned with salt," he becomes despised by the multitude, while he gains nothing from his own nobleness of mind; and if on the other hand he is successful as a preacher, and is overcome by the thought of applause, harm is equally done in turn, both to himself and the multitude, because in his desire for praise he is careful to speak rather with a view to please than to profit.

—John Chrysostom
Treatise Concerning the Christian Priesthood

Devout Conversation Aids Spiritual Progress

Proverbs 12:18; 15:2; 18:21; James 3:5–9

Theme: Friendship, Speech

Bad habits and indifference to spiritual progress do much to remove the guard from the tongue. Devout conversation on spiritual matters, on the contrary, is a great aid to spiritual progress, especially when persons of the same mind and spirit associate together in God.

—Thomas à Kempis
The Imitation of Christ

Do Not Trust Your Own Opinion Too Much

Proverbs 15:22; 18:2; Philippians 2:3

Theme: Humility

Who is so wise as to have perfect knowledge of all things? Therefore trust not too much to your own opinion, but be ready also to hear the opinions of others. Though your own opinion be good, yet if for the love of God you forego it, and follow that of another, you shall the more profit thereby.

—Thomas à Kempis
The Imitation of Christ

Even the Most Devout Experience a Lessening of Fervor

1 Kings 19:9–10

Theme: Discouragement

I have never met a man so religious and devout that he has not experienced at some time a withdrawal of grace and felt a lessening of fervor.

—Thomas à Kempis
The Imitation of Christ

Faith Is Required, Not a Lofty Intellect

Hebrews 10:22–23

Theme: Faith, Education

Faith is required of you, and a sincere life, not a lofty intellect nor a delving into the mysteries of God.

—Thomas à Kempis
The Imitation of Christ

Lead a Dying Life

1 Peter 2:24

Theme: Submission, Death

Realize that you must lead a dying life; the more a man dies to himself, the more he begins to live unto God.

—Thomas à Kempis
The Imitation of Christ

Lovers of the Kingdom, Not the Cross

Matthew 10:38; 16:24; Mark 8:34; 10:21; Luke 9:23

Theme: Discipleship, Kingdom of God

Jesus always has many who love His heavenly kingdom, but few who bear His cross.

—Thomas à Kempis
The Imitation of Christ

Loving Obscurity Before the Spotlight

Matthew 19:30; 20:16; Mark 9:35; 10:31; Luke 13:30

Theme: Leadership, Pride, Humility, Speech

No man appears in safety before the public eye unless he first relishes obscurity. No man is safe in speaking unless he loves to be silent. No man rules safely unless he is willing to be ruled. No man commands safely unless he has learned well how to obey. No man rejoices safely unless he has within him the testimony of a good conscience.

—Thomas à Kempis
The Imitation of Christ

Neglecting Your Soul to Study the Stars

1 Corinthians 8:1; James 4:6

Theme: Education, Wisdom, Reverence, Pride, Humility

Every man naturally desires knowledge; but what good is knowledge without fear of God? Indeed a humble rustic who serves God is better than a proud intellectual who neglects his soul to study the course of the stars. He who knows himself well becomes mean in his own eyes and is not happy when praised by men.

—Thomas à Kempis
The Imitation of Christ

Seek Advice from the Wise and God-Fearing

Proverbs 11:14; 15:22

Theme: Counseling

Do not open your heart to every man, but discuss your affairs with one who is wise and who fears God.

—Thomas à Kempis
The Imitation of Christ

Truth in Scripture, Not Cunning Words

Psalm 119:160; John 17:17

Theme: Scripture, Truth

It is Truth which we must look for in Holy Writ, not cunning of words. All Scripture ought to be read in the spirit in which it was written. We must rather seek for what is profitable in Scripture, than for what ministers to subtlety in discourse.

—Thomas à Kempis
The Imitation of Christ

We Also Have Faults Others Must Endure

Matthew 7:1–5

Theme: Hypocrisy, Judgment, Patience, Mercy

Try to bear patiently with the defects and infirmities of others, whatever they may be, because you also have many a fault which others must endure. If you cannot make yourself what you would wish to be, how can you bend others to your will? We want them to be perfect, yet we do not correct our own faults.

—Thomas à Kempis
The Imitation of Christ

You Can Rest If Your Heart Doesn't Reproach You

Matthew 27:3–5; 1 John 3:19–20

Theme: Guilt, Peace

Sweet shall be your rest if your heart does not reproach you.

—Thomas à Kempis

The Imitation of Christ

Aiming at God's Glory in Everything

1 Chronicles 29:11; Psalm 57:5, 11; 108:5; 113:4

Theme: Work, Service, Obedience, Glory, Presence of God

Wherever man may stand, whatever he may do, to whatever he may apply his hand, in agriculture, in commerce, and in industry, or his mind, in the world of art, and science, he is, in whatever it may be, constantly standing before the face of his God. He is employed in the service of his God, he has strictly to obey his God, and above all, he has to aim at the glory of his God.

—Abraham Kuyper
Calvinism and Religion

Art and the Beauty of Creation

Genesis 1:1; 4:17–22

Theme: Beauty, Creation

If God is and remains Sovereign, then art can work no enchantment except in keeping with the ordinances which God ordained for the beautiful, when He, as the Supreme Artist, called this world into existence. And further, if God is and remains Sovereign, then he also imparts these artistic gifts to whom He will, first even to Cain's, and not to Abel's posterity; not as if art were of Cain, but in order that he who has sinned away the highest gifts should at least, as Calvin so beautifully says, in the lesser gifts of art have some testimony of the divine bounty.

—Abraham Kuyper
Calvinism and Art

Devotion Is a Life Given to God

Ephesians 1:4; Hebrews 12:28

Theme: Commitment

Devotion signifies a life given, or devoted, to God. He, therefore, is the devout man, who lives no longer to his own will, or the way and spirit of the world, but to the sole will of God, who considers God in everything, who serves God in everything, who makes all the parts of his common life parts of piety, by doing everything in the Name of God, and under such rules as are conformable to His glory.

—William Law

A Serious Call to a Devout and Holy Life

Not Pious Because You Didn't Intend It

Exodus 19:8; 24:3; Numbers 32:31; Deuteronomy 5:27; Hebrews 10:23

Theme: Commitment

If you will here stop and ask yourselves why you are not as pious as the primitive Christians were, your own heart will tell you that it is neither through ignorance nor inability, but purely because you never thoroughly intended it.

—William Law

A Serious Call to a Devout and Holy Life

Seeing Afflictions in the Right Light

James 1:2

Theme: Suffering

The sorest afflictions never appear intolerable, but when we see them in a wrong light: when we see them in the hand of God, who dispenses them; when we know that it is our loving Father, who abases and distresses us, our sufferings lose all their bitterness, and our mourning becomes all joy.

—Brother Lawrence

The Practice of the Presence of God

Misfortunes Hardest to Bear Are Those Which Never Come

Ecclesiastes 3:12

Theme: Happiness

Let us be of good cheer … remembering that the misfortunes hardest to bear are those which never come. The world has outlived much, and will outlive a great deal more, and men have contrived to be happy in it.

—James Russell Lowell
Democracy

Justified by Faith, Not Works

Ephesians 2:8–9

Theme: Good Works, Faith, Justification

It is not from works that we are set free by the faith of Christ, but from the belief in works, that is from foolishly presuming to seek justification through works. Faith redeems our consciences, makes them upright, and preserves them, since by it we recognize the truth that justification does not depend on our works, although good works neither can nor ought to be absent, just as we cannot exist without food and drink and all the functions of this mortal body.

—Martin Luther

Concerning Christian Liberty

The Christian Is Free to Serve

1 Corinthians 9:19

Theme: Freedom, Service

A Christian man is the most free lord of all, and subject to none; a Christian man is the most dutiful servant of all, and subject to everyone.

—Martin Luther
Concerning Christian Liberty

Connection Between the Death of Jesus and Destruction of Jerusalem

Matthew 24:1–2; Mark 13:1–2; Luke 21:5–6

Theme: Death of Jesus

What benefit did the Athenians obtain by putting Socrates to death …? Or the people of Samos by the burning of Pythagoras …? Or the Jews [by the murder] of their Wise King, seeing that from that very time their kingdom was driven away [from them]? For with justice did God grant a recompense to the wisdom of [all] three of them. For the Athenians died by famine; and the people of Samos were covered by the sea without remedy; and the Jews, brought to desolation and expelled from their kingdom, are driven away into every land.

—Mara bar Serapion

Letter to his Son

Christ Is Praying for Me

Isaiah 53:12; Luke 22:32; Romans 8:34; Hebrews 7:25

Theme: Jesus, Intercessory Prayer

If I could hear Christ praying for me in the next room, I would not fear a million enemies. Yet the distance makes no difference; He is praying for me.

—Robert Murray McCheyne

Memoir

Christian Everywhere Except Home

Mark 7:9–13

Theme: Hypocrisy

It is the mark of a hypocrite to be a Christian everywhere except at home.

—Robert Murray McCheyne

Sermon 13

"Your Life Preaches All the Week"

1 Timothy 4:16

Theme: Church Leadership, Holiness

Study universal holiness of life. Your whole usefulness depends on this. Your sermon on Sabbath lasts but an hour or two; your life preaches all the week. Remember, ministers are standard-bearers. Satan aims his fiery darts at them. If he can only make you a covetous minister, or a lover of pleasure, or a lover of praise, or a lover of good eating, then he has ruined your ministry forever. ... Take heed to yourself and to your doctrine.

—Robert Murray McCheyne

Sermon 11

Nobody Could Invent Jesus

Luke 1:2; 2 Peter 1:16

Theme: Jesus

Who among his disciples, or among their proselytes, was capable of inventing the sayings ascribed to Jesus, or of imagining the life and character revealed in the Gospels? Certainly not the fishermen of Galilee; as certainly not St. Paul, whose character and idiosyncrasies were of a totally different sort; still less the early Christian writers, in whom nothing is more evident than that the good which was in them was all derived, as they always professed that it was derived, from the higher source.

—John Stuart Mill

Essays on Religion

No Evangelist Better Than the Holy Spirit

Luke 4:18; Acts 19:2; Romans 15:18–19; 1 Peter 1:12

Theme: Holy Spirit, Evangelism

There is not a better evangelist in the world than the Holy Spirit. If the churches would just let Him come in, there would soon be mighty work for Christ.

—Dwight L. Moody
The Holy Spirit and His Work

One Sure Guide to Truth

Psalm 25:5; John 16:13; 2 Timothy 2:15

Theme: Guidance, Scripture, Truth

There is one sure and infallible guide to truth, and therefore one, and only one, corrective for error, and that is the Word of God.

—G. Campbell Morgan

The Spirit of God

The Less We Do, the Less We Desire

Ephesians 6:18; Colossians 4:2; 1 Thessalonians 5:17; 1 Peter 3:7

Theme: Scripture, Prayer, Discipline

In order to enjoy the Word, we ought to continue to read it, and the way to obtain a spirit of prayer, is, to continue praying; for the less we read the Word of God, the less we desire to read it, and the less we pray, the less we desire to pray.

—George Müller

Autobiography: A Million and a Half in Answer to Prayer

"Religion Is Man's Relations to the Divine Being"

2 Peter 1:16

Theme: Revelation, Obedience, Philosophy

The Christian religion is not a theory or speculation about God. It is more than deductions from objective facts concerning his nature and attributes. These are not altogether excluded from Christian theology, but they are not its foundations nor the chief elements of its content. Primarily religion is man's relations to the divine Being. It involves fellowship and obedience on man's part, and self-revelation on God's part. It is a form of experience and of life.

—Edgar Young Mullins
The Christian Religion in Its Doctrinal Expression

Faith and Humility Are One

Habakkuk 2:4; Zephaniah 3:12

Theme: Faith, Pride, Humility

As we see how in their very nature pride and faith are irreconcilably at variance, we shall learn that faith and humility are at root one, and that we never can have more of true faith than we have of true humility.

—Andrew Murray

Humility: The Beauty of Holiness

Absurd to Evangelize by Arguing or Torturing

2 Timothy 2:25; Titus 3:2

Theme: Evangelism

It is as absurd to argue men, as to torture them, into believing.

—John Henry Newman
The Usurpations of Reason

After the Fever of Life, the Beatific Vision

Isaiah 6:3; 1 Thessalonians 4:13; Revelation 20:11

Theme: Death, Heaven, Sabbath

After the fever of life; after wearinesses and sicknesses; fightings and despondings; languor and fretfulness; struggling and failing, struggling and succeeding; after all the changes and chances of this troubled unhealthy state, at length comes death, at length the White Throne of God, at length the Beatific Vision.

—John Henry Newman

Peace in Believing

"Controversy Is Either Superfluous or Hopeless"

Hebrews 11:1; 2 Timothy 2:23

Theme: Conflict, Faith

Half the controversies in the world are verbal ones; and, could they be brought to a plain issue, they would be brought to a prompt termination. Parties engaged in them would then perceive, either that in substance they agreed together, or that their difference was one of first principles. This is the great object to be aimed at in the present age, though confessedly a very arduous one. … When men understand what each other mean, they see, for the most part, that controversy is either superfluous or hopeless.

—John Henry Newman
Faith and Reason, Contrasted as Habits of Mind

Difficult to Rebuke Well

Mark 6:18

Theme: Discipline

It is difficult to rebuke well, that is, at a right time, in a right spirit, and a right manner.

—John Henry Newman

Rebuking Sin

"Lead, Kindly Light"

Psalm 43:3; 119:105; Isaiah 42:16

Theme: Guidance, Faith

Lead, kindly Light, amid the
    encircling gloom,
Lead thou me on!
The night is dark, and I am far
    from home,—
Lead thou me on!
Keep thou my feet! I do not ask to see
The distant scene—one step enough
    for me.

—John Henry Newman
The Pillar of Cloud

Self-Denial Consists in Little Things

Luke 9:23; Romans 13:11

Theme: Discipleship, Discipline

The self-denial which is pleasing to Christ consists in little things. This is plain, for opportunity for great self-denials does not come every day. Thus to take up the cross of Christ is no great action done once for all, it consists in the continual practice of small duties which are distasteful to us.

—John Henry Newman

Self-Denial the Test of Religious Earnestness

Assurance Grows with Experience

Romans 4:13–25; 2 Timothy 1:12

Theme: Assurance, Faith

Assurance grows by repeated conflict, by our repeated experimental proof of the Lord's power and goodness to save; when we have been brought very low and helped, sorely wounded and healed, cast down and raised again, have given up all hope, and been suddenly snatched from danger, and placed in safety; and when these things have been repeated to us and in us a thousand times over, we begin to learn to trust simply to the word and power of God, beyond and against appearances: and this trust, when habitual and strong, bears the name of assurance; for even assurance has degrees.

—John Newton

Private Correspondence

Be On Your Guard After Great Successes

Genesis 9:20–21; 19:30–38; 2 Samuel 11:1–4; 1 Kings 11:1–8

Theme: Temptation, Watchfulness

There are critical times of danger. After great services, honors, and consolations, we should stand upon our guard. Noah, Lot, David, Solomon, fell in these circumstances. Satan is a robber: A robber will not attack a man in going to the bank, but in returning with his pocket full of money.

—John Newton
Personal Conversation

Capable of Three Births

John 3:3–8

Theme: Conversion, Death

Man is made capable of three births: by nature, he enters into the present world; by grace, into spiritual light and life; by death, into glory.

—John Newton

Personal Conversation

Christ Has Been In Our Situation

Isaiah 53:3; 2 Corinthians 5:21; Philippians 3:10

Theme: Suffering, Union with Christ

He knows our sorrows, not merely as he knows all things, but as one who has been in our situation, and who, though without sin himself, endured when upon earth inexpressibly more for us than he will ever lay upon us. He has sanctified poverty, pain, disgrace, temptation, and death, by passing through these states: and in whatever states his people are, they may by faith have fellowship with him in their sufferings, and he will by sympathy and love have fellowship and interest with them in theirs.

—John Newton
Private Correspondence

Christis Represents Us, We Represent Him

2 Corinthians 5:20; Hebrews 7:23–25; 2 Peter 1:4

Theme: Mission

Christ has taken our nature into heaven, to represent *us*; and has left us on earth, with his nature, to represent *him*.

—John Newton
Personal Conversation

Considering Ourselves Righteous by Comparing Ourselves with Others

Romans 3:23; 5:12

Theme: Sin

The generality make out their righteousness by comparing themselves with some others whom they think worse. A woman of the town, who was dying of [sexually transmitted] disease in the Lock Hospital, was offended at a minister speaking to her as a sinner because she had never picked a pocket.

—John Newton
Personal Conversation

Having a Heart Filled with God's Love

Matthew 19:19; 22:39; Mark 12:31; Luke 10:27; John 13:34–35; 15:12–17;
Romans 13:8–9; Galatians 5:14; Hebrews 13:1;
1 John 3:8, 11, 23; 4:7, 11–12; 2 John 5
Theme: Love of God, Love, Mercy

The love of God, as manifested in Jesus Christ, is what I would wish to be the abiding object of my contemplation; not merely to speculate upon it as a doctrine, but so to feel it, and my own interest in it, as to have my heart filled with its effects, and transformed into its resemblance; that, with this glorious Exemplar in my view, I may be animated to a spirit of benevolence, love, and compassion, to all around me; that my love may be primarily fixed upon him who has so loved me, and then, for his sake, diffused to all his children, and to all his creatures.

—John Newton
Private Correspondence

John Newton's Definition of Faith

2 Timothy 1:12

Theme: Faith

This is faith: a renouncing of everything we are apt to call our own, and relying wholly upon the blood, righteousness, and intercession of Jesus.

—John Newton
Private Correspondence

Learning by Walking the Hospital

1 John 3:18

Theme: Education

My course of study, like that of a surgeon, has principally consisted in walking the hospital.

—John Newton

Personal Conversation

"Much Depends on the Way
We Come Into Trouble"

Jonah 1:4–16; Acts 27:14–38

Theme: Suffering

Much depends on the way we come into trouble. Paul and Jonah were both in a storm, but in very different circumstances.

—John Newton

Personal Conversation

No Better Rule of Reading the Scripture

Deuteronomy 17:19

Theme: Scripture

I know not a better rule of reading the Scripture, than to read it through from beginning to end; and, when we have finished it once, to begin it again. We shall meet with many passages which we can make little improvement of, but not so many in the second reading as in the first, and fewer in the third than in the second: provided we pray to him who has the keys to open our understandings, and to anoint our eyes with his spiritual ointment.

—John Newton
Private Correspondence

Providence or Temptation?

What some call providential openings are often powerful temptations. The heart, in wandering, cries, "Here is a way opened before me"; but, perhaps, not to be *trodden*, but *rejected*.

—John Newton
Personal Conversation

Satan Starts Small with Temptations

Matthew 4:1; Mark 1:13; Luke 4:2

Theme: Temptation, Satan

Satan will seldom come to a Christian with a gross temptation. A green log and a candle may be safely left together; but bring a few shavings, then some small sticks, and then larger, and you may soon bring the green log to ashes.

—John Newton
Personal Conversation

Self-Righteousness in Holding Doctrines

1 Corinthians 8:1

Theme: Pride, Legalism

I am afraid there are Calvinists, who, while they account it a proof of their humility that they are willing in words to debase the creature, and to give all the glory of salvation to the Lord, yet know not what manner of spirit they are of. Whatever it be that makes us trust in ourselves that we are comparatively wise or good, so as to treat those with contempt who do not subscribe to our doctrines, or follow our party, is a proof and fruit of a self-righteous spirit. Self-righteousness can feed upon doctrines, as well as upon works.

—John Newton

Private Correspondence

The Analogy of Faith Better Than Systems

Romans 12:6

Theme: Faith, Scripture

There is the analogy of faith: it is a master key, which not only opens particular doors, but carries you through the whole house. But an attachment to a rigid system is dangerous: Luther once turned out the Epistle of St. James because it disturbed his system. I shall preach, perhaps, very usefully upon two opposite texts, while kept apart; but, if I attempt nicely to reconcile them, it is ten to one if I do not begin to bungle.

—John Newton
Personal Conversation

The Highest Attainment We Can Reach

Psalm 51:17

Theme: Humility, Victory

I am persuaded a broken and a contrite spirit, a conviction of our vileness and nothingness, connected with a cordial acceptance of Jesus as revealed in the Gospel, is the highest attainment we can reach in this life.

—John Newton

Private Correspondence

The Unprofitableness of Controversy

Proverbs 29:9; 1 Timothy 6:4; 2 Timothy 2:23; Titus 3:9

Theme: Conflict

I see the unprofitableness of controversy in the case of Job and his friends: for, if God had not interposed, had they lived to this day, they would have continued the dispute.

—John Newton
Personal Conversation

There Is Evil and a Way to Escape It

Habakkuk 1:3; 2 Peter 1:4

Theme: Evil

Many have puzzled themselves about the origin of evil. I observe there is evil, and that there is a way to escape it; and with this I begin and end.

—John Newton
Personal Conversation

"True Religion Is a Habitual Recollection of God and Intention to Serve Him"

Hebrews 12:28

Theme: Service

When some people talk of religion, they mean they have heard so many sermons, and performed so many devotions, and thus mistake the means for the end. But true religion is a habitual recollection of God and intention to serve him; and this turns everything into gold. We are apt to suppose that we need something splendid to evince our devotion, but true devotion equals things: washing plates and cleaning shoes is a high office, if performed in a right spirit.

—John Newton
Personal Conversation

Assurance Without Regard to Circumstances

2 Corinthians 12:2–10; Hebrews 5:7

Theme: Assurance

God sometimes marvelously raises the souls of his saints with some close and near approaches unto them … this is their assurance. But this life is not a season to be always taking wages in. Our work is not yet done; we are not always to abide in this mount; we must down again into the battle—fight again, cry again, complain again. Shall the soul be thought now to have lost its assurance? Not at all. … A man's assurance may be as good, as true, when he lies on the earth with a sense of sin, as when he is carried up to the third heaven with a sense of love and foretaste of glory.

—John Owen

Exposition upon Psalm 130

Beholding Glory by Faith

2 Corinthians 3:18; 5:7

Theme: Faith, Glory

No man shall ever behold the glory of Christ by sight hereafter, who does not in some measure behold it by faith here in this world.

—John Owen

Meditations on the Glory of Christ

Despising the New Birth
John 3:3; 1 John 3:9; 5:1, 4, 18
Theme: Conversion

Let them pretend what they please, the true reason why any despise the new birth is, because they hate a new life. He that cannot endure to live to God will as little endure to hear of being born of God.

—John Owen
Work of the Holy Spirit

Mortification Must Be Done by the Spirit

Romans 8:9–26

Theme: Holy Spirit, Sin, Holiness

All other ways of mortification are vain; all helps leave us helpless. It must be done by the Spirit.

—John Owen

Of the Mortification of Sin

No Death of Sin Without Christ's Death

Romans 8:13; Colossians 3:5

Theme: Death of Jesus, Sin

There is no death of sin without the death of Christ.

—John Owen

Of the Mortification of Sin

We Can Know Experimentally What
We Cannot Know Comprehensively

Ephesians 3:19

Theme: Wisdom

Ephesians 3:19 is a peculiar kind of expression. The meaning is, that we may know that experimentally, which we cannot know comprehensively—that we may know that in its power and effects, which we cannot comprehend in its nature and depths. A weary person may receive refreshment from a spring, who cannot fathom the depths of the ocean from whence it proceeds.

—John Owen

Discourse on Ephesians

We Have No Power of Our Own

2 Chronicles 20:12; John 15:5

Theme: Power of God, Power

We can have no power from Christ unless we live in a persuasion that we have none of our own.

—John Owen

Necessity of Holiness

Faith Not the Contrary of Sight

2 Corinthians 5:7

Theme: Faith

Faith indeed tells what the senses do not tell, but not the contrary of what they see. It is above them, and not contrary to them.

—Blaise Pascal

Thoughts

Fear and Faith

Matthew 8:26; Mark 4:40; Luke 8:25

Theme: Faith, Fear

True fear comes from faith; false fear comes from doubt. True fear is joined to hope, because it is born of faith, and because men hope in the God in whom they believe. False fear is joined to despair, because men fear the God in whom they have no belief. The former fear to lose Him; the latter fear to find Him.

—Blaise Pascal

Thoughts

Give Thanks for God's Revelation

Deuteronomy 29:29; 1 Samuel 3:21; John 21:1

Theme: Revelation, Thankfulness

Instead of complaining that God has hidden Himself, you will give Him thanks for having revealed so much of Himself.

—Blaise Pascal

Thoughts

More Difficult to Be Born or to Be Raised?

Acts 17:32

Theme: Atheism, Resurrection

Atheists—What reason have they for saying that we cannot rise from the dead? What is more difficult, to be born or to rise again; that what has never been should be, or that what has been should be again? Is it more difficult to come into existence than to return to it? Habit makes the one appear easy to us; want of habit makes the other impossible.

—Blaise Pascal

Thoughts

Pascal's Wager

John 11:40; Hebrews 11:6

Theme: Faith

Let us weigh the gain and the loss in wagering that God is. Let us estimate these two chances. If you gain, you gain all; if you lose, you lose nothing. Wager then without hesitation that He is.

—Blaise Pascal

Thoughts

Seeking God Without Jesus

John 1:14–18; Hebrews 1:1–4

Theme: Atheism, Jesus

All who seek God without Jesus Christ, and who rest in nature, either find no light to satisfy them, or come to form for themselves a means of knowing God and serving Him without a mediator. Thereby they fall either into atheism, or into deism, two things which the Christian religion abhors almost equally.

—Blaise Pascal

Thoughts

"The Heart Has Its Reasons"

Jeremiah 17:9

Theme: Sin, Evil, Philosophy

The heart has its reasons, which reason does not know.

—Blaise Pascal

Thoughts

Truth Known by the Heart

2 Timothy 2:25; 3:7

Theme: Truth

We know truth, not only by the reason, but also by the heart.

—Blaise Pascal

Thoughts

Truths That Seem to Contradict

Proverbs 26:4–5; Ecclesiastes 3:1–8

Theme: Truth, Faith

Faith embraces many truths which seem to contradict each other.

—Blaise Pascal

Thoughts

Unless We Love the Truth, We Cannot Know It

2 Thessalonians 2:10

Theme: Truth

Truth is so obscure in these times, and falsehood so established, that unless we love the truth, we cannot know it.

—Blaise Pascal

Thoughts

We Can Only Know Ourselves by Jesus Christ

Jeremiah 17:9; Luke 24:27; John 5:39; Galatians 4:9

Theme: Wisdom, Jesus, Scripture

Not only do we know God by Jesus Christ alone, but we know ourselves only by Jesus Christ. We know life and death only through Jesus Christ. Apart from Jesus Christ, we do not know what is our life, nor our death, nor God, nor ourselves. Thus without the Scripture, which has Jesus Christ alone for its object, we know nothing, and see only darkness and confusion in the nature of God, and in our own nature.

—Blaise Pascal

Thoughts

"We Like to Be Deceived"

Romans 16:18; 1 Thessalonians 2:5

Theme: Honesty

If any have some interest in being loved by us, they are averse to render us a service which they know to be disagreeable. They treat us as we wish to be treated. We hate the truth, and they hide it from us. We desire flattery, and they flatter us. We like to be deceived, and they deceive us.

—Blaise Pascal

Thoughts

Knowing Little About Heaven

1 Corinthians 13:12

Theme: Heaven

Oh! when we meet in heaven, we shall see how little we knew about it on earth.

—Edward Payson

Private communication, a few days before his death

The Need of Tenderness in Ministers

James 1:19–20

Theme: Church Leadership

I never was fit to say a word to a sinner except when I had a broken heart myself; when I was subdued and melted into penitency, and felt as though I had just received pardon to my own soul, and when my heart was full of tenderness and pity. No anger, no anger.

—Edward Payson

A Description of Early Roman Persecution of Christians

Matthew 5:10–12; 13:21; Mark 4:17; Luke 8:13; Hebrews 3:12

Theme: Apostasy, Persecution

The method I have observed towards those who have been brought before me as Christians is this: I asked them whether they were Christians; if they admitted it, I repeated the question twice, and threatened them with punishment; if they persisted, I ordered them to be at once punished: for I was persuaded, whatever the nature of their opinions might be, a contumacious and inflexible obstinacy certainly deserved correction.

—Pliny the Younger

Letter to Emperor Trajan

Early Christian Worship and Persecution

Matthew 5:10–12; 24:9; Luke 21:12; John 15:20;
2 Timothy 3:12; Revelation 2:10

Theme: Worship, Persecution

Christians affirmed the whole of their guilt …was, that they met on a stated day before it was light, and addressed a form of prayer to Christ, as to a divinity, binding themselves by a solemn oath … never to commit any fraud, theft, or adultery, never to falsify their word, nor deny a trust when they should be called upon to deliver it up; after which it was their custom to separate, and then reassemble, to eat in common a harmless meal. … This contagious superstition is not confined to the cities only, but has spread its infection among the neighboring villages and country. Nevertheless, it still seems possible to restrain its progress.

—Pliny the Younger
Letter to Emperor Trajan

"Luke Is a Historian of the First Rank"

Luke 1:1–4

Theme: Scripture

Luke is a historian of the first rank. Not merely are his statements of fact trustworthy; he is possessed of the true historic sense. He fixes his mind on the idea and plan that rules in the evolution of history, and proportions the scale of his treatment to the importance of each incident. He seizes the important and critical events and shows their true nature at greater length, while he touches lightly or omits entirely much that was valueless for his purpose. In short, this author should be placed along with the very greatest of historians.

—William M. Ramsay
Trustworthiness of the New Testament

Luke's Reliability as a Historian

Luke 1:1–4

Theme: Scripture

I set out to look for truth on the borderland where Greece and Asia meet, and found it here. You may press the words of Luke in a degree beyond any other historian's, and they stand the keenest scrutiny and the hardest treatment, provided always that the critic knows the subject and does not go beyond the limits of science and of justice.

—William M. Ramsay

Trustworthiness of the New Testament

The Difference Between Jesus and Socrates

Mark 4:41; Luke 7:49; 8:45; 23:34

Theme: Jesus, Divinity of Jesus, Scripture, Philosophy

Can it be possible that the sacred personage whose history the Scriptures contain should be a mere man? Where is the man, where the philosopher, who could so live and so die without weakness and without ostentation? When Plato describes his imaginary righteous man, loaded with all the punishments of guilt, yet meriting the highest rewards of virtue, he exactly describes the character of Jesus Christ. ...

Peruse the books of philosophers with all their pomp of diction. How meager, how contemptible are they when compared with the Scriptures! The majesty of the Scriptures strikes me with admiration.

—Jean-Jacques Rousseau
On Education, Book Four

Backsliding Starts With Neglect of Prayer

Jeremiah 5:23; 8:5; Matthew 6:6; Luke 5:16

Theme: Apostasy, Prayer

What is the cause of most backsliding? I believe, as a general rule, one of the chief causes is neglect of private prayer. Of course the secret history of falls will not be known till the last day. I can only give my opinion as a minister of Christ and a student of the heart. That opinion is, I repeat distinctly, that backsliding generally first begins with *neglect of private prayer*.

—J. C. Ryle
Practical Religion

Children Born Biased Toward Evil

Proverbs 22:15; 29:15

Theme: Children

Remember children are born with a decided bias toward evil, and therefore if you let them choose for themselves, they are certain to choose wrong. The mother cannot tell what her tender infant may grow up to be—tall or short, weak or strong, wise or foolish: he may be any of these things or not—it is all uncertain. But one thing the mother can say with certainty: he will have a corrupt and sinful heart. It is natural to us to do wrong. … Our hearts are like the earth on which we tread; let it alone, and it is sure to bear weeds.

—J. C. Ryle
The Upper Room

Converted, Yet With Doubts and Fears

Matthew 8:25–26; Mark 4:38–40; Luke 8:24–25

Theme: Conversion, Holiness, Doubt, Fear

Contend to the death for the truth, that no man is a true Christian who is not converted, and is not a holy man. But allow that a man may be converted, have a new heart, and be a holy man, and yet be liable to infirmity, doubts, and fears.

—J. C. Ryle
Holiness

Dislike the Notion of a Second Conversion

John 3:3–6; 2 Corinthians 5:17; Ephesians 4:22–24

Theme: Conversion

I thoroughly dislike the notion of a second conversion.

—J. C. Ryle

Holiness

Don't Expect a Perfect Church

Matthew 3:12

Theme: Church Fellowship and Unity, Second Coming

Before Christ comes it is useless to expect to see a perfect Church.

—J. C. Ryle
Practical Religion

Faith Is to Prayer as Feather Is to Arrow

Mark 11:24; Luke 18:1; 1 Timothy 2:8

Theme: Faith, Prayer

Faith is to prayer what the feather is to the arrow: Without it prayer will not hit the mark.

—J. C. Ryle

Practical Religion

Fire Quenched by Money

Luke 12:15

Theme: Greed, Money, Wealth

Nothing I am sure has such a tendency to quench the fire of religion as the possession of money.

—J. C. Ryle

Practical Religion

Glorying in the Cross of Christ

Galatians 6:14; 1 John 2:2; 4:10

Theme: Death of Jesus, Atonement

Let us serve him faithfully as our Master. Let us obey Him loyally as our King. Let us study His teaching as our Prophet. Let us walk diligently after Him as our Example. Let us look anxiously for Him as our coming Redeemer of body as well as soul. But above all, let us prize Him as our sacrifice, and rest our whole weight on His death as an atonement for sin. Let His blood be more precious in our eyes every year we live. Whatever else we glory in about Christ, let us glory above all things in His cross.

—J. C. Ryle

Expository Thoughts on John, Volume One

Inability to Discern Doctrinal Differences

Proverbs 15:14; 1 Thessalonians 5:21

Theme: Wisdom, False Teaching

Inability to distinguish differences in doctrine is spreading far and wide, and so long as the preacher is "clever" and "earnest," hundreds seem to think it must be all right, and call you dreadfully "narrow and uncharitable" if you hint that he is unsound!

—J. C. Ryle

Holiness

Let Our Rule of Faith Be the Bible

Exodus 24:3; Deuteronomy 17:19; Psalm 119:160; Acts 17:10–12

Theme: Scripture

Let us read the Bible regularly, daily, and with fervent prayer, and become familiar with its contents. Let us receive nothing, believe nothing, follow nothing, which is not in the Bible, nor can be proved by the Bible. Let our rule of faith, our touchstone of all teaching, be the written Word of God.

—J. C. Ryle
Knots Untied, Chapter 17

No Sudden Holiness

Ephesians 2:21

Theme: Holiness

The theory of a sudden, mysterious transition of a believer into a state of blessedness and entire consecration at one mighty bound, I cannot receive. It appears to me to be a man-made invention; and I do not see a single plain text to prove it in Scripture.

—J. C. Ryle

Holiness

Prayer and Sinning

Matthew 6:5–13; Mark 11:25

Theme: Prayer, Sin

Praying and sinning will never live together in the same heart. Prayer will consume sin, or sin will choke prayer.

—J. C. Ryle

Practical Religion

The Bible Applied to the Heart

Psalm 119:9; Luke 10:26; John 5:39; 17:17; 2 Timothy 3:16–17

Theme: Scripture, Holy Spirit, Holiness, Righteousness, Good Works

---

The Bible applied to the heart by the Holy Ghost is the chief means by which men are built up and established in the faith, after their conversion. It is able to cleanse them, to sanctify them, to instruct them in righteousness, and to furnish them thoroughly for all good works.

—J. C. Ryle
Practical Religion

The Elect Distinguished by Holy Lives

Romans 12:1; 1 Thessalonians 4:7

Theme: Election, Holiness

The names and number of the elect are a secret thing, no doubt, which God has wisely kept in His own power, and not revealed to man. It is not given to us in this world to study the pages of the book of life, and see if our names are there. But if there is one thing clearly and plainly laid down about election, it is this: that elect men and women may be known and distinguished by holy lives.

—J.C. Ryle

Holiness

"Neither a Borrower Nor a Lender Be"

Proverbs 22:7

Theme: Borrowing, Debt

Neither a borrower, nor a lender be;
For loan oft loses both itself and friend,
And borrowing dulls the edge
   of husbandry.

—William Shakespeare

Hamlet

"Poor and Content Is Rich"

Philippians 4:11–12; 1 Timothy 6:6, 8; Hebrews 13:5

Theme: Contentment

Poor and content is rich, and rich enough.

—William Shakespeare

Othello

"The Devil Can Cite Scripture for His Purpose"

Matthew 4:6; Luke 4:9–11

Theme: Satan, Scripture

The devil can cite Scripture for his purpose.

—William Shakespeare
The Merchant of Venice

The Singeing Effects of Anger

Deuteronomy 32:35; Romans 12:19; Hebrews 10:30

Theme: Anger, Revenge

Heat not a furnace for your foe so hot
That it do singe yourself.

—William Shakespeare

Henry VIII

Dying Well the Action of Life

1 Corinthians 15:31; Philippians 1:23–24

Theme: Death

To die well is the action of the whole life.

—Richard Sibbes

Christ Is Best

Afflictions: Christ's Mallet and Chisel

Colossians 1:12

Theme: Suffering, Holiness

Afflictions cannot sanctify us, except as they are used by Christ as his mallet and his chisel. Our joys and our efforts cannot make us ready for heaven apart from the hand of Jesus who fashions our hearts aright, and prepares us to be partakers of the inheritance of the saints in light.

—Charles Spurgeon
Christ Glorified as the Builder of His Church

Arguing About Food, and Not Eating It

Philippians 4:2; 1 Timothy 1:4; 2 Timothy 2:23; Titus 3:9

Theme: Conflict

Two learned doctors are angrily discussing the nature of food, and allowing their meal to lie untasted, while a simple countryman is eating as heartily as he can of that which is set before him. The religious world is full of quibblers, critics, and sceptics, who, like the doctors, fight over Christianity without profit either to themselves or others; those are far happier who imitate the farmer and feed upon the Word of God, which is the true food of the soul. Luther's prayer was, "From nice questions the Lord deliver us."

—Charles Spurgeon
The Sword and Trowel: 1865

"Believing Does Not Come by Trying"

1 Thessalonians 5:9; 2 Timothy 2:10; 3:15

Theme: Faith

Believing does not come by trying. If a person were to make a statement of something that happened this day, I should not tell him that I would try to believe him. If I believed in the truthfulness of the man who told the incident to me and said that he saw it, I should accept the statement at once. If I did not think him a true man, I should, of course, disbelieve him; but there would be no trying in the matter. Now, when God declares that there is salvation in Christ Jesus, I must either believe Him at once, or make Him a liar.

—Charles Spurgeon
All of Grace

"Calvinism Is the Gospel"

1 Corinthians 2:2

Theme: Election, Gospel

I have my own private opinion that there is no such thing as preaching Christ and Him crucified, unless we preach what nowadays is called Calvinism. It is a nickname to call it Calvinism; Calvinism is the gospel, and nothing else.

—Charles Spurgeon
Christ Crucified

Children Capable of Receiving Christ

Matthew 19:14; Mark 10:14; Luke 18:16

Theme: Children, Salvation

Those children who are of years sufficient to sin, and to be saved by faith, have to listen to the gospel and to receive it by faith: and they can do this, God the Holy Spirit helping them. There is no doubt about it, because great numbers have done it. I will not say at what age children are first capable of receiving the knowledge of Christ, but it is much earlier than some fancy; and we have seen and known children who have given abundant evidence that they have received Christ and have believed in Him at a very early age.

—Charles Spurgeon
Come, Ye Children

Choose Neither Evil

Romans 12:21; 1 Thessalonians 5:22

Theme: Evil

Of two evils, choose neither.

—Charles Spurgeon
Jude's Doxology

Depression Often Follows a Great Victory

1 Kings 19:1–10

Theme: Discouragement, Depression, Victory

When at last a long-cherished desire is fulfilled, when God has been glorified greatly by our means, and a great triumph achieved, then we are apt to faint. It might be imagined that amid special favors our soul would soar to heights of ecstasy, and rejoice with joy unspeakable, but it is generally the reverse. The Lord seldom exposes his warriors to the perils of exultation over victory; he knows that few of them can endure such a test, and therefore dashes their cup with bitterness.

—Charles Spurgeon
The Minister's Fainting Fits

Dust on Your Bibles

Hosea 8:12

Theme: Scripture

There is dust enough on some of your Bibles to write "damnation" with your fingers.

—Charles Spurgeon
The Bible

Election and Freedom Not in Conflict

John 15:16–17; Ephesians 1:3–14

Theme: Election, Freedom, Salvation

There are two great truths which from this platform I have proclaimed for many years. The first is that salvation is free to every man who will have it; the second is that God gives salvation to a people whom he has chosen; and these truths are not in conflict with one another in the least degree.

—Charles Spurgeon
Thou Art Now the Blessed of the Lord

Faith and Obedience Are Bound Together

2 Thessalonians 1:3; James 2:14–26

Theme: Faith, Obedience, Good Works

Faith and obedience are bound up in the same bundle. He that obeys God, trusts God, and he that trusts God, obeys God. He that is without faith is without works; and he that is without works is without faith. Do not oppose faith and good works to one another, for there is a blessed relationship between them; and if you abound in obedience your faith shall grow exceedingly.

—Charles Spurgeon
The Necessity of Growing Faith

Giving Thanks for the Incarnation
Any Day of the Year

Luke 2:7

Theme: Birth of Jesus

We venture to assert, that if there be any day in the year, of which we may be pretty sure that it was not the day on which the Savior was born, it is the twenty-fifth of December. Nevertheless ... since it is lawful, and even laudable, to meditate upon the incarnation of the Lord upon any day in the year, it cannot be in the power of other men's superstitions to render such a meditation improper for today. Regarding not the day, let us, nevertheless, give God thanks for the gift of his dear son.

—Charles Spurgeon
Joy Born at Bethlehem

Giving Yourself to the Lord, but Not the Church?

2 Corinthians 8:5; Hebrews 10:25

Theme: Church Fellowship and Unity, Obedience

There are some who say, "Well, I have given myself to the Lord, but I do not intend to give myself to any church." Now, why not? "Because I can be a Christian without it." Now, are you quite clear about that? You can be as good a Christian by disobedience to your Lord's commands as by being obedient? … You believe that if you were to do an act which has a tendency to destroy the visible Church of God, you would be as good a Christian as if you did your best to build up that Church? I do not believe it, sir! Nor do you either. You have not any such a belief; it is only an excuse for something else.

—Charles Spurgeon
Joining the Church

God Enters the Heart with a Master-Key

Psalm 105:37; John 3:3–8; Ephesians 4:22–24

Theme: Conversion

God does not violate the human will when he saves men: they are not converted against their will, but their will itself is converted. The Lord has a way of entering the heart, not with a crowbar, like a burglar, but with a master-key, which he gently inserts in the lock, and the bolt flies back, the door opens, and he enters.

—Charles Spurgeon
A Stanza of Deliverance

"God Never Does Really Forsake Us"

Psalm 22:1; Matthew 27:46; Mark 15:34

Theme: Suffering, Discouragement

There are seasons when the brightness of our Father's smile is eclipsed by clouds and darkness. But let us remember that God never does really forsake us. It is only a seeming forsaking with us, but in Christ's case it was a real forsaking. God only knows how much we grieve, sometimes, at a little withdrawal of our Father's love; but the real turning away of God's face from his Son—who shall calculate how deep the agony which it caused him when he cried, "My God, my God, why hast thou forsaken me?"

—Charles Spurgeon

Cries from the Cross

God Never Would Have Chosen Me Afterwards

Romans 9:11; Ephesians 1:4

Theme: Election

I believe the doctrine of election, because I am quite sure that if God had not chosen me I should never have chosen him;
and I am sure he chose me before I was born, or else he never would have chosen me afterwards.

—Charles Spurgeon
The Sword and Trowel: 1874

God's Smile of Love in Grief

Psalm 147:16–18

Theme: Grief, Sovereignty of God, Love of God, Death

We see his smile of love even when others see nothing but the black hand of Death smiting our best beloved.

—Charles Spurgeon

Frost and Thaw

"Have I Written in the Snow?"

2 Corinthians 4:18

Theme: Work

Here is a good searching question for a man to ask himself as he reviews his past life: Have I written in the snow? Will my lifework endure the lapse of years and the fret of change? Has there been anything immortal in it that will survive the speedy wreck of all terrestrial things? The boys inscribe their names in capitals in the snow, and in the morning's thaw the writing disappears; will it be so with my work, or will the characters which I have carved outlast the brazen tablets of history? Have I written in the snow?

—Charles Spurgeon
Feathers for Arrows

He Carries the Burden Also

Matthew 10:38; 11:28–30; 16:24; Mark 8:34; Luke 9:23

Theme: Discipleship

The heaviest end of the cross lies ever on his shoulders. If he bids us carry a burden, he carries it also.

—Charles Spurgeon

The Statute of David for the Sharing of the Spoil

Letting the Gospel Lion Out

Isaiah 55:11; Acts 19:20; Romans 15:19–20;
1 Corinthians 1:17; 4:19–20; 15:1–2

Theme: Gospel, Evangelism

A great many learned men are defending the gospel. … Yet I always notice that, when there are most books of that kind, it is because the gospel itself is not being preached. Suppose a number of persons were to take it into their heads that they had to defend a lion, a full-grown king of beasts! There he is in the cage, and here come all the soldiers of the army to fight for him. Well, I should suggest to them … that they should kindly stand back, and open the door, and let the lion out! I believe that would be the best way of defending him, for he would take care of himself; and the best "apology" for the gospel is to let the gospel out.

—Charles Spurgeon
Christ and His Co-Workers

Lies Go Around the World While Truth Pulls Its Boots On

Matthew 5:11; 1 Peter 2:12

Theme: Slander, Truth, Honesty, Complaining

It is a great deal easier to set a story afloat than to stop it. If you want truth to go around the world you must hire an express train to pull it; but if you want a lie to go around the world, it will fly. It is as light as a feather, and a breath will carry it. It is well said in the old proverb, "A lie will go around the world while truth is pulling its boots on." Nevertheless, it does not injure us; for if light as a feather it travels as fast, its effect is just about as tremendous as the effect of down when it is blown against the walls of a castle. It produces no damage whatever, on account of its lightness and littleness.

—Charles Spurgeon
Joseph Attacked by the Archers

Love Others as Christ Loves You

Matthew 19:19; 22:39; Mark 12:31; Luke 10:27;
John 13:34–35; 15:12–17; Romans 13:8–9; Galatians 5:14;
Hebrews 13:1; 1 John 3:8, 11, 23; 4:7, 11–12; 2 John 5

Theme: Love of God, Love

Christ loved you before you loved him. … He loved you though you insulted him, though you despised him and rebelled against him. He has loved you right on, and never ceased to love you. He has loved you in your backslidings and loved you out of them. He has loved you in your sins, in your wickedness and folly. His loving heart was still eternally the same, and he shed his heart's blood to prove his love for you. He has given you what you want on earth, and provided for you an habitation in heaven.

Now Christian, your religion claims from you that you should love as your Master loved. How can you imitate him, unless you love too?

—Charles Spurgeon
Love Thy Neighbor

More Reading the Bible, More Astonishment

Psalm 119:148

Theme: Scripture

The more you read the Bible, and the more you meditate upon it, the more you will be astonished with it. He who is but a casual reader of the Bible, does not know the height, the depth, the length, and breadth of the mighty meanings contained in its pages.

—Charles Spurgeon
Christ Our Passover

More Time Reading the News Than God's Word

Deuteronomy 6:6–9; 11:18–21; Hosea 8:12

Theme: Scripture

I venture to say that the bulk of Christians spend more time in reading the newspaper than they do in reading the Word of God.

—Charles Spurgeon

The Unkept Vineyard

Most Grand Truths Learned by Trouble

Job 23:10; Isaiah 48:10; Jonah 2:9; 2 Corinthians 12:7–9

Theme: Suffering, Education

M ost of the grand truths of God have to be learned by trouble; they must be burned into us with the hot iron of affliction, otherwise we shall not truly receive them.

—Charles Spurgeon
Salvation of the Lord

No Crown-Wearing Without Cross-Bearing

Matthew 27:32; Mark 15:21; Luke 14:27; 23:26

Theme: Discipleship

There are no crown-wearers in heaven who were not cross-bearers here below.

—Charles Spurgeon
Gleanings Among the Sheaves

No Mistake in the Scriptures

Psalm 12:6; Matthew 22:29

Theme: Scripture

I do not hesitate to say that I believe that there is no mistake whatever in the original Holy Scriptures from beginning to end. There may be, and there are, mistakes of translation; for translators are not inspired; but even the historical facts are correct. Doubt has been cast upon them here and there, and at times with great show of reason—doubt which it has been impossible to meet for a season; but only give space enough, and search enough, and the stones buried in the earth cry out to confirm each letter of Scripture.

—Charles Spurgeon
The Bible Tried and Proved

Nobody Outgrows Scripture

2 Timothy 3:16; Hebrews 4:12

Theme: Scripture

Nobody ever outgrows Scripture; the Book widens and deepens with our years.

—Charles Spurgeon
The Talking Book

Not Keeping the Honey for Yourself

John 1:40–46

Theme: Evangelism

I will not believe that you have tasted of the honey of the gospel if you can eat it all yourself. True grace puts an end to all spiritual monopoly.

—Charles Spurgeon
The First Five Disciples

Not Saved by Right Doctrine

Romans 3:24

Theme: Salvation, Faith, Good Works

You can be no more saved by believing right doctrine than you can by doing right actions.

—Charles Spurgeon
Justification by Grace

Orthodox in Creed, but Heterodox in Life

Matthew 7:21–23; Luke 6:46

Theme: Hypocrisy, Character, Faith, Discipleship

We care little for those who are orthodox Christians in creed if it is clear that they are heterodox in life.

—Charles Spurgeon

Flowers from a Puritan's Garden

Owing Grandeur to Difficulties

Job 23:10; Isaiah 48:10; 2 Corinthians 4:17; Revelation 7:14

Theme: Suffering

Many men owe the grandeur of their lives to their tremendous difficulties.

—Charles Spurgeon

The Sword and Trowel: 1884

Perfectly God and Perfectly Man

Hebrews 2:17

Theme: Humanity of Jesus, Divinity of Jesus

Remember, Christ was not a deified man, neither was he a humanized God. He was perfectly God, and at the same time perfectly man, made like unto his brethren in all things.

—Charles Spurgeon
The Matchless Mystery

Prayer Is the Key to Understanding Scripture

1 Corinthians 2:12–13

Theme: Scripture, Holy Spirit, Prayer

When we have no commentator or minister, we have still the Holy Spirit; and let me tell you a little secret: whenever you cannot understand a text, open your Bible, bend your knee, and pray over that text; and if it does not split into atoms and open itself, try again. If prayer does not explain it, it is one of the things God did not intend you to know, and you may be content to be ignorant of it. Prayer is the key that opens the cabinets of mystery. Prayer and faith are sacred picklocks that can open secrets, and obtain great treasures.

—Charles Spurgeon
The Holy Ghost: The Great Teacher

Preferring to Believe in an Efficacious Limited Atonement

Isaiah 53:10

Theme: Atonement, Election

I had rather believe a limited atonement that is efficacious for all men for whom it was intended, than a universal atonement that is not efficacious for anybody, except the will of man be joined with it.

—Charles Spurgeon
The Death of Christ

Pride in Being a Worse Backslider
Than Other People

Romans 10:13; Philippians 3:19; 4:4

Theme: Pride

There is a certain breed of Calvinists, whom I do not envy, who are always jeering and sneering as much as ever they can at the full assurance of faith. … But why is it that they do this?… Because there is a pride within them—a conceit which is fed on rottenness, and sucks marrow and fatness out of putrid carcasses. And what, say you, is the object of their pride? Why, the pride of being able to boast of a deep experience—the pride of being a blacker, grosser and more detestable backslider than other people. … A more dangerous, because a more deceitful pride than this is not to be found. It has all the elements of self-righteousness in it.

—Charles Spurgeon
Full Assurance

Some Truth in Both Calvinism and Arminianism

Acts 2:23; 4:27–28; Romans 8:29–30; Ephesians 1:3–12

Theme: Election, Truth, Philosophy

When a Calvinist says that all things happen according to the predestination of God, he speaks the truth, and I am willing to be called a Calvinist; but when an Arminian says that, when a man sins, the sin is his own, and that, if he continues in sin, and perishes, his eternal damnation will lie entirely at his own door, I believe that he also speaks the truth, though I am not willing to be called an Arminian. … There is some truth in both these systems of theology; the mischief is that, in order to make a human system appear to be complete, men ignore a certain truth, which they do not know how to put into the scheme which they have formed.

—Charles Spurgeon
The Way of Wisdom

Summary of Archibald Alexander's Theology

1 Timothy 1:15

Theme: Salvation

The late venerable and godly Dr. Archibald Alexander, of Princeton, United States, had been a preacher of Christ for sixty years, and a professor of divinity for forty. He died on 22nd October, 1851. On his deathbed, he was heard to say to a friend, "All my theology is reduced to this narrow compass—Jesus Christ came into the world to save sinners."

—Charles Spurgeon

Feathers for Arrows

Taking Issue with the Bible's Chapter Divisions

Matthew 9:35–10:4

Theme: Scripture

I feel vexed with the fellow who chopped the Bible up into chapters. … I have heard that he did the most of his carving of the New Testament between London and Paris, and rough work he made of it. Surely he was chaptering the Gospel of Matthew while he was crossing the Channel, for he has divided it in such queer places.

—Charles Spurgeon
Harvest Men Wanted

The Cold Water of Persecution

Matthew 5:10–12; Acts 8:1; 1 Peter 4:13–14

Theme: Persecution

The cold water of persecution is often thrown on the church's face to fetch her to herself when she is in a swoon of indolence or pride.

—Charles Spurgeon

Feathers for Arrows

"The Doctrine of Resurrection Is Full of Joy to the Bereaved"

John 11:24

Theme: Resurrection

The doctrine of the resurrection is full of joy to the bereaved. It clothes the grave with flowers, and wreathes the tomb with unfading laurel. The sepulcher shines with a light brighter than the sun, and death grows fair, as we say, in full assurance of faith, "I know that my brother shall rise again." Rent from the ignoble shell the pearl is gone to deck the crown of the Prince of Peace; buried beneath the sod the seed is preparing to bloom in the King's garden.

—Charles Spurgeon

Feathers for Arrows

The World Is a Bog

Matthew 13:22; Mark 4:19; Colossians 2:8

Theme: Watchfulness

Queen Elizabeth I once said to a courtier, "They pass best over the world who trip over it quickly; for it is but a bog: if we stop, we sink."

—Charles Spurgeon

Feathers for Arrows

Thinking You're a Scholar When You're Not

1 Corinthians 4:6–13

Theme: Pride, Humility

Quintilian said of some in his time that they might have become excellent scholars had they not been so persuaded of their scholarship already. Grant, most gracious God, that I may never hold so high an opinion of my own spiritual health as to prevent my being in very deed full of your grace and fear!

—Charles Spurgeon

Feathers for Arrows

Who Limits the Atonement?

Matthew 20:28

Theme: Atonement, Death of Jesus, Election, Salvation

We are often told that we limit the atonement of Christ, because we say that Christ has not made a satisfaction for all men, or all men would be saved. Now, our reply to this is that, on the other hand, our opponents limit it. ... You say that Christ did not die so as to infallibly secure the salvation of anybody. ... We say Christ so died that he infallibly secured the salvation of a multitude that no man can number who through Christ's death not only may be saved, but are saved, must be saved and cannot by any possibility run the hazard of being anything but saved.

—Charles Spurgeon
Particular Redemption

"Worldly Ease Is a Great Foe to Faith"

Luke 12:13–21; Romans 5:3–5

Theme: Comfort, Suffering, Faith

Worldly ease is a great foe to faith; it loosens the joints of holy valor, and snaps the sinews of sacred courage. The balloon never rises until the cords are cut: affliction does this sharp service for believing souls. While the wheat sleeps comfortably in the husk it is useless to man, it must be threshed out of its resting-place before its value can be known. Trial plucks the arrow of faith from the repose of the quiver, and shoots it against the foe.

—Charles Spurgeon
A Mystery! Saints Sorrowing and Jesus Glad!

Claudius Banishes the Jews from Rome

Acts 18:2

Theme: Persecution

He [Claudius] banished from Rome all the Jews, who were continually making disturbances at the instigation of one Chrestus.

—Suetonius

The Lives of the Twelve Caesars

Record of Nero's Persecution of Christians

Matthew 24:9; Luke 21:12; John 15:20; 2 Timothy 3:12; Revelation 2:10

Theme: Persecution

He [Nero] likewise inflicted punishments on the Christians, a sort of people who held a new and impious superstition.

—Suetonius

The Lives of the Twelve Caesars

Cannot Know Ourselves Without Knowing God

Jeremiah 17:9; Galatians 4:9

Theme: Wisdom, Humility, Purity

We shall never be able to know ourselves, except we endeavor to know God. By considering His greatness, we discover our own baseness; by contemplating His purity, we discover our own filthiness, and beholding His humility, we shall discover how far we are from being truly humble.

—Teresa of Ávila

The Interior Castle

Faith Is Not Belief Without Evidence

Romans 4:3, 19–21; Titus 1:2

Theme: Faith

Faith is not belief without evidence. It is belief on the very best of evidence, the word of Him who cannot lie. Faith is so rational that it asks no other evidence than this all-sufficient evidence. To ask other evidence than the word of Him "who cannot lie" is not "rationalism," but consummate irrationalism.

—R. A. Torrey
What the Bible Teaches

Gaining the Victory Before the Battle

Matthew 26:41; Mark 14:38; Luke 22:46

Theme: Prayer, Discipline, Spiritual Warfare

The reason why many fail in the battle is because they wait until the hour of battle. The reason why others succeed is because they have gained their victory on their knees long before the battle came.

—R. A. Torrey

How to Succeed in the Christian Life

Trajan's Reply to Pliny

Matthew 5:10–12; 13:21; Mark 4:17; Luke 8:13; Hebrews 3:12

Theme: Persecution

You have adopted the right course, my dearest Secundus, in investigating the charges against the Christians who were brought before you. It is not possible to lay down any general rule for all such cases. Do not go out of your way to look for them. If indeed they should be brought before you, and the crime is proved, they must be punished; with the restriction, however, that where the party denies he is a Christian, and shall make it evident that he is not, by invoking our gods, let him (notwithstanding any former suspicion) be pardoned upon his repentance.

—Emperor Trajan
Letter to Pliny the Younger

Not Faith That Saves, but Christ Through Faith

Ephesians 2:8–9; 1 Peter 1:9

Theme: Faith, Salvation

It is not, strictly speaking, even faith in Christ that saves, but Christ that saves through faith. The saving power resides exclusively, not in the act of faith or the attitude of faith or the nature of faith, but in the object of faith; and in this the whole biblical representation centres, so that we could not more radically misconceive it than by transferring to faith even the smallest fraction of that saving energy which is attributed in the Scriptures solely to Christ Himself.

—B. B. Warfield

Biblical Doctrines

Afflicted on Two Sides

Job 5:17; 2 Timothy 2:12

Theme: Suffering, Temptation, Satan

The godly have some good in them, therefore the devil afflicts them; and some evil in them, therefore God afflicts them.

—Thomas Watson

A Body of Practical Divinity

"A Reading People Will Always Be a Knowing People"

Ezra 8:1–12; 2 Timothy 4:13

Theme: Wisdom, Speech

It cannot be that the people should grow in grace, unless they give themselves to reading. A reading people will always be a knowing people. A people who talk much will know little.

—John Wesley
Letter, 8 November 1790

All Have a Claim to Our Courtesy

Deuteronomy 15:7; Proverbs 14:31; 19:17; Matthew 25:40

Theme: Mercy, Humility, Poverty

See that you are courteous toward all men. It matters not, in this respect, whether they are high or low, rich or poor, superior or inferior to you. No, not even whether good or bad, whether they fear God or not. Indeed, the mode of showing your courtesy may vary, as Christian prudence will direct; but the thing itself is due to all; the lowest and the worst have a claim to our courtesy.

—John Wesley
On Pleasing All Men

Always in Haste, but Never in a Hurry

Psalm 131:2

Theme: Stress, Work

Though I am always in haste, I am never in a hurry; because I never undertake any more work than I can go through with perfect calmness of spirit.

—John Wesley
Letter to Francis Wanley

Be Not Swallowed Up in Books

1 Corinthians 8:1; 13:2

Theme: Love, Wisdom

Beware you be not swallowed up in books: An ounce of love is worth a pound of knowledge.

—John Wesley

Letter to Joseph Benson

Exacting More from Yourself Than Others

Philippians 2:14; James 5:9

Theme: Complaining

The longer I live, the larger allowances I make for human infirmities. I exact more from myself, and less from others.

—John Wesley

Letter, 25 January 1762

Following the Bible in All Things

Psalm 119:57, 101, 105, 158

Theme: Scripture

My ground is the Bible. Yes, I am a Bible-bigot. I follow it in all things, both great and small.

—John Wesley

Journal, 2 June 1766

Gain All You Can, Save All You Can, Give All You Can

Matthew 6:19; 1 Timothy 6:18

Theme: Money, Giving

Give all your money to God. You have no pretense for laying up treasure upon earth. While you "gain all you can," and "save all you can," "give all you can," that is, all you have.

—John Wesley

Thoughts on Marriage and the Single Life

Give Me 100 Preachers

Matthew 16:18

Theme: Church Leadership, Commitment, Kingdom of God

Give me one hundred preachers who fear nothing but sin, and desire nothing but God, and I care not a straw whether they be clergymen or laymen, such alone will shake the gates of hell, and set up the kingdom of heaven upon earth.

—John Wesley

Letter to Alexander Mather

Giving Everything Over 10 Pounds

Matthew 19:21; 1 John 3:17

Theme: Giving

If I leave behind me ten pounds (above my debts, and my books, or what may happen to be due on account of them), you and all mankind bear witness against me, that I lived and died a thief and a robber.

—John Wesley
An Earnest Appeal

Growing by Degrees

1 Corinthians 3:6; Ephesians 4:15–16;
2 Thessalonians 1:3; 1 Peter 2:2; 2 Peter 3:18

Theme: Holiness

Everyone, though born of God in an instant, and sanctified in an instant, yet undoubtedly grows by slow degrees.

—John Wesley

Letter, 27 June 1760

Hardly Sure of Anything Except the Bible

Psalm 119:160; Matthew 24:35; John 17:17

Theme: Truth, Scripture

After having sought for truth, with some diligence, for half a century, I am, at this day, hardly sure of anything but what I learn from the Bible.

—John Wesley
The Good Steward

"Let Me Be Nothing"

John 3:30; 1 Corinthians 15:28

Theme: Pride, Humility

O, beware, do not seek to be something!
Let me be nothing, and Christ be all in all!

—John Wesley

Letter to Francis Asbury

Love God and Your Household

Matthew 22:37–40; Mark 12:30–31; Luke 10:27–28

Theme: Family, Love

God is the first object of our love: Its next office is, to bear the defects of others. And we should begin the practice of this amidst our own household.

—John Wesley
A Plain Account of Christian Perfection

"May We Not Love Alike?"

1 John 4:7–11

Theme: Love, Church Fellowship and Unity

Although a difference in opinions or modes of worship may prevent an entire external union; yet need it prevent our union in affection? Though we cannot think alike, may we not love alike? May we not be of one heart, though we are not of one opinion?

—John Wesley
Catholic Spirit

"O Give Me That Book!"

1 Timothy 4:13; 2 Timothy 3:15–16

Theme: Scripture

I want to know one thing—the way to heaven; how to land safe on that happy shore. God himself has condescended to teach the way: For this very end he came from heaven. He has written it down in a book. O give me that book! At any price, give me the book of God! I have it: Here is knowledge enough for me. Let me be *homo unius libri* [a man of one book].

—John Wesley
Preface to Sermons

Passion and Prejudice Govern the World

Leviticus 19:15; 1 Timothy 5:21

Theme: Prejudice, Conflict

Passion and prejudice govern the world; only under the name of reason. It is our part, by religion and reason joined, to counteract them all we can.

—John Wesley

Letter to Joseph Benson

"Preach Faith Till You Have It"

Romans 10:8–9

Theme: Faith

Immediately it struck into my mind, "Leave off preaching. How can you preach to others, who have not faith yourself?" I asked Böhler whether he thought I should leave it off or not. He answered, "By no means." I asked, "But what can I preach?" He said, "Preach faith till you have it; and then, because you have it, you will preach faith."

—John Wesley

Journal, 4 March 1738

Self-Denial the Life of Piety

Matthew 16:24; Mark 8:34; Luke 9:23; Romans 8:13; Galatians 5:24

Theme: Discipline, Sacrifice

Self-denial of all kinds is the very life and soul of piety.

—John Wesley

Redeeming the Time

Sure of What God Has Revealed

Matthew 24:35

Theme: Humility, Truth, Revelation

When I was young, I was sure of everything: In a few years, having been mistaken a thousand times, I was not half so sure of most things as I was before. At present I am hardly sure of anything but what God has revealed to man.

—John Wesley
A Letter to the Editor of the London Magazine

"Use No Constraint in Matters of Religion"

Luke 14:23; Galatians 2:14; 6:12

Theme: Power, Freedom, Truth, Love

Never dream of forcing men into the ways of God. Think yourself, and let think. Use no constraint in matters of religion. Even those who are farthest out of the way never compel to come in by any other means than reason, truth, and love.

—John Wesley

The Nature of Enthusiasm

Your Duty Is to Save Souls

James 5:20

Theme: Evangelism, Mission

You have nothing to do but to save souls. Therefore spend and be spent in this work. And go always, not only to those that need you, but to those that need you most. Observe: It is not your business to preach so many times, and to take care of this or that society; but to save as many souls as you can; to bring as many sinners as you possibly can to repentance, and with all your power to build them up in that holiness without which they cannot see the Lord.

—John Wesley
Personal Conversation

Zeal for Souls Beats Desire for Comfort

1 Corinthians 9:16

Theme: Evangelism, Comfort

What marvel the devil does not love field-preaching! Neither do I: I love a commodious room, a soft cushion, a handsome pulpit. But where is my zeal, if I do not trample all these underfoot in order to save one more soul?

—John Wesley

Journal, 24 June 1759

Accepting Those Who Love Jesus Sincerely

John 17:20–23; Romans 14:19

Theme: Peace, Church Fellowship and Unity

If I see a man who loves the Lord Jesus in sincerity, I am not very solicitous to what outward communion he belongs. The kingdom of God, I think, does not consist in any such thing.

—George Whitefield

Letter, 16 January 1740

Christ in the Head, Not in the Heart

Matthew 18:3

Theme: Legalism, Character, Conversion

If a person is what the world calls an honest moral man, if he does justly, and loves a little mercy, is now and then good-natured, reaches out his hand to the poor, receives the sacrament once or twice a year, and is outwardly sober and honest; the world looks upon such an one as a Christian indeed, and doubtless we are to judge charitably of every such person. There are many likewise, who go on in a round of duties, a model of performances, that think they shall go to heaven; but if you examine them, though they have a Christ in their heads, they have no Christ in their hearts.

—George Whitefield
Marks of a True Conversion

Dead Ministry Makes Dead People

1 Timothy 4:16

Theme: Church Leadership, Love, Love of God

A dead ministry will always make a dead people, whereas if ministers are warmed with the love of God themselves, they cannot but be instruments of diffusing that love among others.

—George Whitefield

Letter to the Students of Cambridge and Newhaven

George Whitefield's Conversion

Matthew 11:28–30; Romans 6:6

Theme: Conversion

I found and felt in myself, that I was delivered from the burden that had so heavily oppressed me. The spirit of mourning was taken from me, and I knew what it was truly to rejoice in God my Savior. For some time I could not avoid singing psalms wherever I was; but my joy became gradually more settled. Thus were the days of my mourning ended: after a long night of desertion and temptation, the star, which I had seen at a distance before, began to appear again: the day-star arose in my heart.

—George Whitefield
A Brief and Summary Account of My Temptations

God and Man Happy Together Again

Romans 5:11; 2 Corinthians 5:18–19

Theme: Divinity of Jesus, Humanity of Jesus, Reconciliation

He was truly God, and therefore could satisfy; he was truly man, and therefore could obey and suffer in our stead. He was God and man in one person, that God and man might be happy together again.

—George Whitefield
What Think Ye of Christ?

"On the Full Stretch for God"

2 Kings 10:29–31; Philippians 3:13

Theme: Obedience

I am never better than when I am on the full stretch for God.

—George Whitefield

Journal, 5 March 1738

Renewal Cannot Be Accomplished in a Day

2 Corinthians 5:17; Ephesians 4:17–24

Theme: Conversion, Revival

The renewal of our natures is a work of great importance. It is not to be done in a day. We have not only a new house to build up, but an old one to pull down.

—George Whitefield

Letter, 6 March 1735

Expecting to Be Christians Without Working

Matthew 16:24; Mark 8:34; Luke 9:23; 14:26–27, 33; John 15:8

Theme: Discipleship

No one expects to attain to the height of learning, or arts, or power, or wealth, or military glory, without vigorous resolution, and strenuous diligence, and steady perseverance. Yet we expect to be Christians without labor, study, or inquiry. This is the more preposterous, because Christianity is a revelation from God, and not the invention of man, discovering to us new relations, with their correspondent duties; containing also doctrines, motives, and precepts peculiar to itself; we cannot reasonably expect to become proficient in it by the accidental intercourses of life.

—William Wilberforce

A Practical View of the Prevailing Religious System of Professed Christians

"The Child Is Father of the Man"

Proverbs 22:6

Theme: Children

The Child is father of the Man.

—William Wordsworth

My Heart Leaps Up

Index of Biblical Verses

Index of Preaching Themes

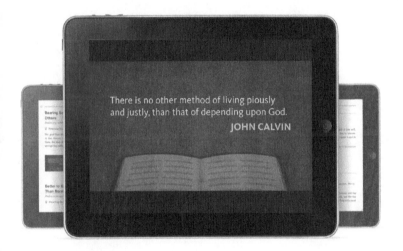

CPSIA information can be obtained at www.ICGtesting.com
Printed in the USA
LVOW01s0536060214

372593LV00003B/4/P